Crochet
COMPENDIUM™

the ultimate collection of crochet techniques

edited by Connie Ellison

credits

EDITOR Connie Ellison
ART DIRECTOR Brad Snow
PUBLISHING SERVICES DIRECTOR Brenda Gallmeyer

ASSOCIATE EDITOR Judy Crow
ASSISTANT ART DIRECTOR Nick Pierce
COPY SUPERVISOR Deborah Morgan
COPY EDITOR Amanda Scheerer
TECHNICAL EDITOR Shirley Brown

PRODUCTION ARTIST SUPERVISOR Erin Augsburger
COVER & BOOK DESIGN Greg Smith
GRAPHIC ARTISTS Jessi Butler, Minette Collins Smith
PRODUCTION ASSISTANTS Marj Morgan, Judy Neuenschwander

PHOTOGRAPHY SUPERVISOR Tammy Christian
PHOTOGRAPHY Scott Campbell, Matthew Owen
PHOTO STYLISTS Martha Coquat, Tammy Liechty, Tammy Steiner

Library of Congress Control Number: 2011900807
ISBN: 978-1-59217-341-9

**HOUSE of
WHITE
BIRCHES**
PUBLISHERS
SINCE 1947

1 2 3 4 5 6 7 8 9

contents

bead crochet

These beading basics are a perfect start for the beginner. Beading is a great way to embellish your crochet designs.

BEADS ON A CROCHETED CHAIN

Before crocheting a beginning chain, string beads on yarn. Make slip knot in yarn and work several chain stitches.

To place a bead in the next chain stitch, push bead into place against the last chain stitch made (see Photo A). Bring yarn over hook on other side of bead (see Photo B) and pull through loop on hook.

Bead will fall to back of chain (see Photo C).

Beads may be worked into every chain stitch or spaced with several chain stitches between beads (see Photo D).

BEADS ON SINGLE CROCHET

String beads onto yarn. Make a chain of desired length to begin or work into a previous row of stitches.

On a beginning chain, work single crochet stitches in 2nd and 3rd chain stitches from hook.

To place a bead in the next single crochet, insert hook in next chain stitch and pull loop through. Push bead into place against chain stitch being worked into (see Photo E).

Bring yarn over hook on other side of bead and pull through both loops on hook.

Bead will fall to back of single crochet *(see Photo F)*.

Work single crochet stitches in same manner in stitches of previous rows or rounds.

Beads may be worked into every single crochet or spaced with stitches between beads.

When the piece is completed, the side with the beads is the right side of piece.

BEADS ON DOUBLE CROCHET

The bead in a double crochet stitch can rest on either the right side or wrong side of the piece depending on when you push the bead into place.

This allows you to crochet back and forth in rows, beading every row, while still having all the beads fall to the right side of fabric.

DOUBLE CROCHET WITH BEAD ON RIGHT SIDE

String beads on yarn. Make chain of desired length to begin or work into a previous row of stitches.

Work several double crochet stitches.

For a bead in the next double crochet stitch, yarn over as you would normally begin a double crochet, push a bead into place so that it is positioned on top of the crochet hook *(see Photo G)*. Insert hook into stitch, pull loop through, yarn over, pull through 2 loops, making sure the bead is captured in this yarn over and is on the top of the crochet *(see Photo H)*. Yarn over and pull through last 2 loops *(see Photo I)*.

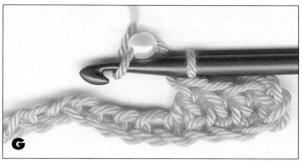

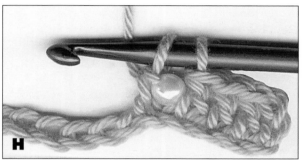

DOUBLE CROCHET WITH BEAD ON WRONG SIDE

String beads on yarn. Make chain of desired length to begin or work into a previous row of stitches.

Yarn over, insert hook into stitch, pull loop through, push bead into place so that it is positioned at the back, next to the loop just made *(see Photo J)*.

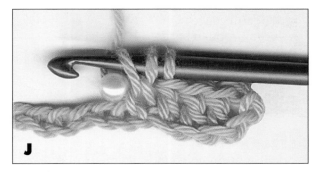

Bring yarn over hook and pull through 2 loops making sure the bead is captured in this yarn over and is on the back of the crochet (*see Photo K*).

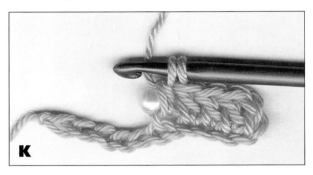

Yarn over and pull through 2 loops (*see Photo L*).

When alternating rows of beads placed on the right side and wrong side of the work, the slant of the rows of beads with alternate. One row will slant to the left and the next row will slant to the right. ∎

bead crochet
beaded market tote

DESIGN BY **NANCY NEHRING**

SKILL LEVEL

INTERMEDIATE

FINISHED SIZE
12 inches tall x 14½ inches wide, excluding Handle

MATERIALS
- 48-lb hemp cord (200g per ball): 3 balls
- Size H/8/5mm crochet hook or size needed to obtain gauge
- 10mm wooden beads: 540
- Fingernail polish or cyanoacrylate glue
- Stitch markers

GAUGE
13 sts = 4 inches

PATTERN NOTES
Work in continuous rounds, do not turn or join unless otherwise stated.

Mark first stitch of round.

Before finishing first ball of hemp, dip end of 2nd ball into fingernail polish or cyanoacrylate glue, shape into a point and let dry. This stiffens end to make bead stringing easier. String beads on 2nd ball.

Join with slip stitch as indicated unless otherwise stated.

INSTRUCTIONS

TOTE
BODY
Rnd 1 (RS): Use palm (*knife*) grip on crochet hook as the hemp needs a firm hand, ch 30, sc in 2nd ch from hook and in each of next 27 chs, 3 sc in last ch, working on opposite side of ch, sc in each of next 28 chs, 3 sc in next ch, do not join (*see Pattern Notes*). (*62 sc*)

Rnd 2: *Sc in each sc across to 2nd sc of next

3-sc group, 3 sc in 2nd sc, rep from * once, sc in next sc. (*66 sc*)

Rnd 3: *Sc in each sc across to next 3-sc group, 2 sc in each of next 3 sc (*mark first sc of this 6-sc group*), rep from * once, sc in next sc. (*72 sc*)

Rnd 4: *Sc in each sc across to marked sc of next 6-sc group, 2 sc in marked sc, sc in next sc (*mark this sc*), 2 sc in next sc, sc in next sc, 2 sc in next sc, rep from * once, sc in each sc across to first sc. (*78 sc*)

Rnd 5: *Sc in each sc across to next marked sc, 2 sc in marked sc (*mark first sc*), [sc in next sc, 2 sc in next sc] twice, rep from * once, sc in each sc across to first sc. (*84 sc*)

Rnd 6: *Sc in each sc across to next marked sc, 2 sc in marked sc, [sc in next sc, 2 sc in next sc] twice, rep from * once, sc in each sc across to first sc. (*90 sc*)

Rnd 7: Sc in back lp (*see Stitch Guide*) of each sc around.

Rnd 8: Sc in each sc around.

Rnds 9–16: Sc in each sc around. See Pattern Notes for beginning new ball. At end of rnd 16, sl 2 additional sts.

Rnd 17: Ch 2, *slide bead into place next to hook, ch with bead (*see Bead Crochet on page 4*), sk next sc, hdc in next sc, rep from * around ending with ch around bead, sl st in 2nd ch of beg ch-2.

Rnds 18–28: Rep rnd 17.

Rnd 29: Sc in each sc around.

Rnds 30–33: Rep rnd 29.

Rnd 34: Sc in each sc around, ch 1. Set side.

HANDLES
GETTING STARTED
From 3rd ball of hemp, cut 242-inch length and 254-inch length. Tie ends of shorter length tog and coil into 5 even lps. Rep with longer length.

Place first coil at top edge of Tote with ch 1 of rnd 34 in front of coil and yarn end at back of

work. Work sc of following rnd over coil and into sc of rnd 34, keeping coil on top of rnd.

Rnd 35: Sc in each of next 22 sc, work 80 sc over coil only, sk next 23 sc on rnd 34, working over coil and into sc, sc in each of next 22 sc, work 80 sc over coil only, join (*see Pattern Notes*) in beg ch-1 sp.

Place rem coil at top of previous rnd and work all sc over coil.

Rnd 36: Ch 1, sk next sc, sc in each of next 20 sc, sk next sc, sc in each of next 80 sc, sk next sc, sc in each of next 20 sc, sk next sc, sc in each of last 80 sc, join in beg ch-1 sp. Fasten off.

FINISHING
Steam Tote heavily.

Block to shape, using four 1-lb cans placed in a line to block the bottom of the Tote. Let dry. ■

bead crochet
beaded blossom

DESIGN BY **NANCY NEHRING**

SKILL LEVEL

EASY

FINISHED SIZE
About 1½ inches in diameter

MATERIALS
- Size 10 crochet cotton:
  10 yds color of choice
- Size 7/1.65mm steel crochet hook or size needed to obtain gauge
- Size 24 tapestry needle
- Size 6/0 assorted color beads: 18
- Stitch marker
- Pin back or barrette (optional)

GAUGE
13 sts = 4 inches

PATTERN NOTES
Work in continuous rounds, do not turn or join unless otherwise stated.

Mark first stitch of round.

Join with slip stitch as indicated unless otherwise stated.

Flower may be sewn to a pin back or barrette when completed.

INSTRUCTIONS

FLOWER
Rnd 1 (RS): String beads onto cotton using tapestry needle, ch 4, sl st in first ch to form ring, ch 1, [sc with bead *(see Bead Crochet on page 4)*] 6 times, do not join *(see Pattern Notes)*. *(6 sc with beads)*

Rnd 2: 2 sc with beads in each sc around. *(12 sc with beads)*

Rnd 3: [Ch 3, sk next sc, sc in next sc] 6 times, turn, having beads to front of work.

Rnd 4: (Sc, hdc, dc, 3 tr, dc, hdc, sc) in each ch-3 sp around, join *(see Pattern Notes)* in beg sc. Fasten off. ■

broomstick lace

By using a size 50 broomstick lace pin or knitting needle and a crochet hook, you can create an open, lacy fabric.

BASIC TECHNIQUE

Begin with a crocheted foundation chain or row of stitches, do not turn work.

Hold the broomstick pin in your left hand and the crochet hook in your right hand like a knife.

For each loop, working from left to right, insert the hook in the stitch on the previous row, pull up a long loop and place it over the pin (see Photo A), pull the loop snug but not tight, repeat until the designated number of loops are on the pin.

To **single crochet (sc)** in loops, at beginning of row, pull loop up to height of row or make a chain to match height of row, insert hook through center of designated number of loops at same time, usually 5 (see Photo B) and remove pin, yarn over and pull through loops, then complete as sc stitch, make the designated number of sc stitches in each group of loops in this manner.

Increases can be made by going through fewer loops as you work the single crochet row or by working extra single crochet stitches into the group of loops (see Photo C).

Decreases can be made by going through more loops as you work the single crochet row or by working fewer single crochet stitches into the group of loops (see Photo D).

broomstick lace
dishcloth

DESIGN BY **ANN WHITE**

SKILL LEVEL

EASY

FINISHED SIZE
10 x 10½ inches

MATERIALS
- Medium (worsted) weight cotton yarn:
  3 oz/150 yds/85g pink
  1 oz/50 yds/28g yellow
- Size G/6/4mm crochet hook or size needed to obtain gauge
- Size 24 tapestry needle
- Size 50/25mm broomstick lace pin

4 MEDIUM

GAUGE
4 sc = 1 inch

INSTRUCTIONS

DISHCLOTH
Row 1: With pink, ch 41, sc in 2nd ch from hook and in each ch across, do not turn. *(40 sc)*

Rows 2–9: Working left to right, slip last lp on hook onto broomstick pin, working this row in back lps *(see Stitch Guide)*, sk first st, [insert hook in next sc, yo, pull lp through st and slip onto broomstick pin *(see Illustration 1)*] across, do not turn, slip first 5 lps from broomstick

pin onto hook, yo, pull lp through all 5 lps on hook *(see Illustration 2)*, ch 1, 5 sc in same 5-lp group *(see Illustration 3)*, [slip next 5 lps from broomstick pin onto hook, yo, pull lp through 5 lps on hook, yo, pull through 2 lps on hook *(sc made)*, 4 sc in same 5-lp group] across, do not turn. At end of last row, fasten off.

EDGING
Join yellow with sc in back lp of first st on right-hand side, sc in back lp of each st across, sc in end of each sc and 5 dc around 5 strands at end of each row across, working in starting ch on opposite side of row 1, sc in each ch across, sc in end of each sc and 5 dc around 5 strands at end of each row across, join with sl st in beg sc. Fasten off. ■

Illus. 1

Illus. 2
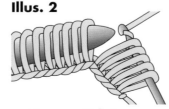

Illus. 3
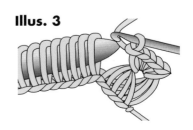

Broomstick Lace

beret & scarf

DESIGNS BY **YVONNE RENEE BARNES**

SKILL LEVEL

EASY

FINISHED SIZES

Beret: 11½ inches in diameter, head opening 5 inches unstretched

Scarf: 9¾ inches wide x 52 inches long

MATERIALS

- Medium (worsted) weight cotton yarn:
  14 oz/700 yds/397g blue
- Size I/9/5.5mm crochet hook or size needed to obtain gauge
- Tapestry needle
- Size 50/25mm broomstick lace pin or knitting needle

4 MEDIUM

GAUGE

3 broomstick lace cluster rep = 3½ inches; 3 pattern rows = 5½ inches

PATTERN NOTES

Join with slip stitch as indicated unless otherwise stated.

When removing loops from pin or knitting needle, be sure that loops do not get pulled out or twisted before working single crochet into them. The first single crochet of row of single crochet that is worked will lock the loops at beginning of row.

Beret requires 6 ounces of yarn and Scarf requires 8 ounces of yarn.

INSTRUCTIONS

SCARF

Row 1: Ch 33, sc in 2nd ch from hook, sc in each ch across, turn. *(32 sc)*

Row 2: Ch 2, sc in each sc across, when last st is formed, pull up lp and place on pin or knitting needle *(see Broomstick Lace on page 9)*, turn.

Row 3: Pull up lp in each sc across, placing each lp on pin or knitting needle as work progresses, turn. *(32 lps)*

Row 4: Ch 2, after slipping all lps off pin or knitting needle or slipping off 4 at a time and working through the center of 4 lps, work 4 sc through the center of the 4 lps, continue to work 4 sc in the center of each 4-lp group across, turn. *(8 groups of 4 lps)*

Row 5: Ch 2, sc in each sc across, turn.

Row 6: Ch 2, sc in each sc across, when last st is formed, pull up lp and place on pin or knitting needle, turn.

Rows 7–114: [Rep rows 3–6 consecutively] 27 times.

Rows 115 & 116: Rep rows 3 and 4.

Row 117: Ch 2, sc in each sc across. Fasten off.

With steam iron, block lightly.

BERET

Row 1: Ch 89, sc in 2nd ch from hook, sc in each ch across, turn. *(88 sc)*

Row 2: Ch 2, sc in each sc across, when last st is formed, pull up lp and place on pin or knitting needle *(see Broomstick Lace on page 9)*, turn.

Row 3: Pull up lp in each sc across, placing each lp on pin or knitting needle as work progresses, turn. *(88 lps)*

Row 4: Ch 2, after slipping all lps off pin or knitting needle or slipping off 4 at a time and working through center of 4 lps, work 4 sc through center of 4 lps, continue to work 4 sc in the center of each 4-lp group across, turn. *(22 groups of 4 lps)*

Row 5: Ch 2, sc in each sc across, turn.

Row 6: Ch 2, sc in each sc across, when last st is formed, pull up lp and place on pin or knitting needle, turn.

Row 7: Rep row 3.

Row 8: Rep row 4.

Row 9: Rep row 5.

Row 10: Ch 2, [sc in each of next 20 sc, sc dec *(see Stitch Guide)* in next 2 sc] 4 times, when last st is formed, pull up lp and place on pin or knitting needle, turn. *(84 sc)*

Row 11: Rep row 3.

Row 12: Ch 2, after slipping all lps off pin or knitting needle or slipping off 4 at a time and working through center of 4 lps, work 4 sc through center of 4 lps, continue to work 4 sc in the center of each 4-lp group across, turn. *(21 groups of 4 lps)*

Row 13: Ch 2, [sc in each of next 19 sc, sc dec in next 2 sc] 4 times, turn. *(80 sc)*

Row 14: Ch 2, [sc in each of next 18 sc, sc dec in next 2 sc] 4 times, when last st is formed, pull up lp and place on pin or knitting needle. *(76 sc)*

Row 15: Rep row 3. *(76 lps)*

Row 16: Ch 2, after slipping all lps off pin or knitting needle or slipping off 4 at a time and working through center of 4 lps, work 2 sc through center of the 4 lps, continue to work 2 sc in center of each 4-lp group across, turn. *(19 groups of 4 lps, 38 sc)*

Row 17: Ch 2, sc in next sc, [sc dec in next 2 sc] 18 times, sc in last sc, turn. *(20 sc)*

Row 18: Ch 2, sc in each sc across, turn.

Row 19: Rep row 3. *(20 lps)*

Row 20: Ch 2, after slipping all lps off pin or knitting needle or slipping off 4 at a time and working through center of 4 lps, work 2 sc through center of 4 lps, continue to work 2 sc in center of each 4-lp group across, turn. *(5 groups of 4 lps, 10 sc)*

Row 21: Ch 2, sc in each sc across, turn. *(10 sc)*

Row 22: Ch 2, [sc dec in next 2 sc] 5 times, turn. *(5 sc)*

Row 23: Ch 2, [sc dec in next 2 sc] twice, sc in last sc. Leaving 18-inch length, fasten off.

With tapestry needle, stitch through the last row of sc to gather top of Beret closed, beg to seam the Beret, stitching in the end rows of sc and extending length of yarn along the broomstick lp rows. Stitch to the end of the seam.

BERET UNDERSIDE

Rnd 1: Working in starting ch on opposite side of row 1, join with sc in first ch, sc in each ch around, join *(see Pattern Notes)* in beg sc. *(88 sc)*

Rnd 2: Ch 2, sc in each of first 9 sc, sc dec in next 2 sc, [sc in each of next 9 sc, sc dec in next 2 sc] 7 times, join in 2nd ch of beg ch-2. *(80 sc)*

Rnd 3: Ch 2, sc in each of first 8 sc, sc dec in next 2 sc, [sc in each of next 8 sc, sc dec in next 2 sc] 7 times, join in 2nd ch of beg ch-2. *(72 sc)*

Rnd 4: Ch 1, sc in each of first 4 sc, sc dec in next 2 sc, [sc in each of next 4 sc, sc dec in next 2 sc] 11 times, join in beg sc. *(60 sc)*

Rnd 5: Ch 1, sc in each of first 4 sc, sc dec in next 2 sc, [sc in each of next 4 sc, sc dec in next 2 sc] 9 times, join in beg sc. *(50 sc)*

Rnd 6: Ch 1, sc in each of first 8 sc, sc dec in next 2 sc, [sc in each of next 8 sc, sc dec in next 2 sc] 4 times, join in beg sc. Fasten off. *(45 sc)*

With steam iron, block lightly. ■

TIPS & HELPFUL HINTS

You will normally work the same number of single crochet stitches in each group of loops as there are loops in the group.

Corners will lay square if you work half the single crochet stitches through the group of loops, then chain about 4 or so chains and work the remainder of the single crochet stitches through the same loops. On the next row, pull up a loop in each chain and in each single crochet stitch.

crocheting doilies

To make stunning doilies, you need only a steel crochet hook, some crochet cotton and a tapestry needle. To give your doilies a more finished look, you will also need blocking and starching supplies.

STEEL HOOKS

Steel hooks range in size from 00 (large) to 16 (very small) and are 5 inches long, which is shorter than the typical aluminum or plastic hooks. Their shape is different from other crochet hooks. There is the throat, then the shank, and after the shank, the steel begins to widen again before it reaches the finger grip (see Illustration 1).

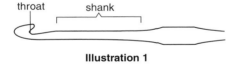

Illustration 1

When crocheting, it is important that the stitches do not slide beyond the shank as this will cause a loose tension and alter the gauge.

THREAD

Thread comes in many sizes: from very fine crochet cotton (sizes 80 and 100), used for lace making and tatting, to sizes 10 and 20 used for doilies, tablecloths and bedspreads. The larger the number the thinner the thread.

BEGINNING A DOILY

Besides the usual crochet stitches, which are found in our Crochet Basics section beginning on page 103, the 2 techniques that you need to know are how to join a chain into a circle and how to join the end of a round to the beginning of the same round.

To practice, chain 6. Insert hook through the first chain you made (next to the slip knot, see Illustration 2).

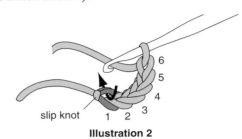

Illustration 2

Hook the thread and pull it through the chain and through the loop on the hook, you have now joined the 6 chains into a circle or ring. This is the way most doilies are started.

Now, chain 3 and work 11 double crochet stitches into the center of the circle. To join round, insert the hook in the 3rd ch of the beginning chain-3 (see Illustration 3), hook thread and pull it through the chain and through the loop on the hook. You have joined the round.

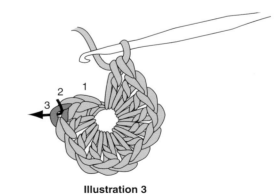

Illustration 3

BLOCKING INFORMATION

Blocking means "setting" the finished doily into its final size and shape.

To do this, wash the doily carefully by hand using a mild soap if necessary and rinse well in warm water. Spread the wet doily out on a flat padded surface, having the right side facing up.

Smooth the doily out to the correct size, having the design properly aligned with all picots, loops, etc., open. If necessary, use rustproof pins to hold edges in place. Let dry thoroughly before removing pins.

STARCHING INFORMATION
If you want your doily to have a stiffer shape, it will be necessary to starch the doily before blocking it. To do this you will need the following supplies:

1. A commercial stiffening solution or white craft glue thoroughly mixed with an equal amount of water.

2. A plastic bag that locks across the top for soaking the doily.

3. A sheet of Styrofoam brand *(our preference)* or a piece of corrugated cardboard to use as a pinning board.

4. Plastic wrap to cover pinning board so doily can be easily removed.

After assembling the supplies, wash doily as described under Blocking Information.

Pour prepared stiffening solution into plastic bag. Immerse doily in solution and let soak 1 minute.

Remove and press out excess solution. Do not squeeze—doily should be very wet, but there should be no solution in the decorative holes (dab with dry paper towel to correct this).

Place doily on covered pinning board and pin as described under Blocking Information. ∎

crocheting doilies
pineapple fantasy doily

SKILL LEVEL

INTERMEDIATE

FINISHED SIZE
20 inches in diameter

MATERIALS
- Size 10 crochet cotton: 450 yds white
- Size 7/1.65mm steel crochet hook or size needed to obtain gauge

GAUGE
8 tr = 1 inch

PATTERN NOTES
Chain-4 at beginning of row or round counts as first treble crochet unless otherwise stated.

Join with slip stitch as indicated unless otherwise stated.

SPECIAL STITCHES
Beginning shell (beg shell): Ch 4, (2 tr, ch 3, 3 tr) in same place.

Shell: (3 tr, ch 3, 3 tr) as indicated in instructions.

Small picot (sm picot): Ch 4, sl st in top of st just worked.

Beginning double shell (beg double shell): Ch 4, (2 tr, {ch 3, 3 tr} twice) in same place.

Double shell: (3 tr, {ch 3, 3 tr} twice) as indicated in instructions.

Large picot (lg picot): Ch 8, sl st in 5th ch from hook.

INSTRUCTIONS

DOILY

Rnd 1 (RS): Ch 8, sl st in first ch to form ring, ch 4 *(see Pattern Notes)*, 23 tr in ring, join *(see Pattern Notes)* in 4th ch of beg ch-4. *(24 tr)*

Rnd 2: Ch 4, 2 tr in same ch, *ch 2, sk next tr**, 3 tr in next tr, rep from * around, ending last rep at **, join in 4th ch of beg ch-4.

Rnd 3: Sl st in next tr, ch 4, (tr, ch 3, 2 tr) in same tr, *ch 1, sk next ch-2 sp** and next tr, (2 tr, ch 3, 2 tr) in next tr, rep from * around, ending last rep at **, join in 4th ch of beg ch-4.

Rnd 4: Sl st in next tr and in next ch-3 sp, ch 7 *(counts as a tr and a ch-3 sp)*, (tr, ch 3, tr) in same ch sp, ch 3, sk next ch-1 sp, *(tr, {ch 3, tr} twice) in next ch-3 sp, ch 3, sk next ch-1 sp, rep from * around, join in 4th ch of beg ch-7.

Rnd 5: Sl st in next ch sp and in next tr, beg shell *(see Special Stitches)* in same st, *ch 3, sk next ch-3 sp, sc in next ch-3 sp, ch 3**, sk next ch-3 sp, shell *(see Special Stitches)* in next tr, rep from * around, ending last rep at **, join in 4th ch of beg ch-4. *(12 shells)*

Rnd 6: Sl st in each of next 2 tr and in next ch-3 sp, ch 1, sc in same ch sp, *ch 6, sk next ch-3 sp, tr in next sc, ch 6, sk next ch-3 sp**, sc in ch-3 sp of next shell, rep from * around, ending last rep at **, join in beg sc.

Rnd 7: Ch 1, sc in first sc, *ch 4, sk next ch-6 sp, shell in next tr, ch 4, sk next ch-6 sp**, sc in next sc, rep from * around, ending last rep at **, join in beg sc.

Rnd 8: Ch 12 (*counts as first tr and ch-8*), sk next ch-4 sp, sc in ch-3 sp of next shell, *ch 8, sk next ch-4 sp**, tr in next sc, ch 8, sk next ch-4 sp, sc in ch-3 sp of next shell, rep from * around, ending last rep at **, join in 4th ch of beg ch-12.

Rnd 9: Beg shell in same ch as joining, *ch 6, sk next ch-8 sp, tr in next sc, sm picot (*see Special Stitches*), ch 6, sk next ch-8 sp**, shell in next tr, rep from * around, ending last rep at **, join in 4th ch of beg ch-4.

Rnd 10: Sl st in each of next 2 tr and in next ch-3 sp, beg shell in same sp, *ch 4, sk next ch-6 sp, 6 tr in next picot (*base of pineapple*), ch 4, sk next ch-6 sp**, shell in ch-3 sp of next shell, rep from * around, ending last rep at **, join in 4th ch of beg ch-4.

Rnd 11: Sl st in each of next 2 tr and in next ch-3 sp, beg shell in same sp, *ch 4, sk next ch-4 sp, sc in next tr, [ch 4, sc in next tr] 5 times, ch 4, sk next ch-4 sp**, shell in ch sp of next shell, rep from * around, ending last rep at **, join in 4th ch of beg ch-4.

Rnd 12: Sl st in each of next 2 tr and in next ch-3 sp, beg shell in same sp, *ch 4, sk next ch-4 sp, sc in next ch-4 sp, [ch 4, sc in next ch-4 sp] 4 times, ch 4, sk next ch-4 sp**, shell in ch sp of next shell, rep from * around, ending last rep at **, join in 4th ch of beg ch-4.

Rnd 13: Sl st in each of next 2 tr and in next ch-3 sp, beg shell in same sp, *ch 5, sk next ch-4 sp, sc in next ch-4 sp, [ch 4, sc in next ch-4 sp] 3 times, ch 5, sk next ch-4 sp**, shell in ch sp of next shell, rep from * around, ending last rep at **, join in 4th ch of beg ch-4.

Rnd 14: Sl st in each of next 2 tr and in next ch-3 sp, beg double shell (*see Special Stitches*) in same sp, *ch 6, sk next ch-5 sp, sc in next ch-4 sp, [ch 4, sc in next ch-4 sp] twice, ch 6, sk next ch-5 sp**, double shell (*see Special Stitches*) in ch sp of next shell, rep from * around, ending last rep at **, join in 4th ch of beg ch-4.

Rnd 15: Sl st in each of next 2 tr and in next ch-3 sp, beg shell in same sp, *lg picot (*see Special Stitches*), ch 3, shell in next ch-3 sp, ch 6, sk next ch-6 sp, sc in next ch-4 sp, ch 4, sc in next ch-4 sp, ch 6, sk next ch-6 sp**, shell in next ch-3 sp, rep from * around, ending last rep at **, join in 4th ch of beg ch-4.

Rnd 16: Sl st in each of next 2 tr and in next ch-3 sp, beg shell in same sp, *ch 4, 7 tr in next picot (*base of pineapple*), ch 4, shell in ch sp of next shell, ch 6, sk next ch-6 sp, sc in next ch-4 sp, ch 6, sk next ch-6 sp**, shell in ch sp of next shell, rep from * around, ending last rep at **, join in 4th ch of beg ch-4.

Rnd 17: Sl st in each of next 2 tr and in next ch-3 sp, beg shell in same sp, *ch 4, sk next ch-4 sp, sc in next tr, [ch 4, sc in next tr] 6 times, ch 4, sk next ch-4 sp, shell in ch sp of next shell, ch 6, sk next ch-6 sp, sc in next sc, ch 6, sk next ch-6 sp**, shell in ch sp of next shell, rep from * around, ending last rep at **, join in 4th ch of beg ch-4.

Rnd 18: Sl st in each of next 2 tr and in next ch-3 sp, beg shell in same sp, *ch 5, sk next ch-4 sp, sc in next ch-4 sp, [ch 4, sc in next ch-4 sp] 5 times, ch 5, sk next ch-4 sp, shell in ch sp of next shell, sk next 2 ch-6 sps**, shell in ch sp of next shell, rep from * around, ending last rep at **, join in 4th ch of beg ch-4.

Rnd 19: Sl st in each of next 2 tr and in next ch-3 sp, beg shell in same sp, *ch 5, sk next ch-5 sp, sc in next ch-4 sp, [ch 4, sc in next ch-4 sp] 4 times, ch 5, sk next ch-5 sp, shell in ch sp of next shell, ch 1**, shell in ch sp of next shell, rep from * around, ending last rep at **, join in 4th ch of beg ch-4.

Rnd 20: Sl st in each of next 2 tr and in next ch-3 sp, beg shell in same sp, *ch 5, sk next ch-5 sp, sc in next ch-4 sp, [ch 4, sc in next ch-4 sp] 3 times, ch 5, sk next ch-5 sp, shell in ch sp of next shell, lg picot, ch 3**, shell in next shell, rep from * around, ending last rep at **, join in 4th ch of beg ch-4.

Rnd 21: Sl st in each of next 2 tr and in next ch-3 sp, beg shell in same sp, *ch 5, sk next ch-5 sp, sc in next ch-4 sp, [ch 4, sc in next ch-4 sp] twice, ch 5, sk next ch-5 sp, shell in ch sp of next shell, ch 3, 7 tr in next picot (*base of pineapple*), ch 3**, shell in ch sp of next shell, rep from * around, ending last rep at **, join in 4th ch of beg ch-4.

Rnd 22: Sl st in each of next 2 tr and in next ch-3 sp, beg shell in same sp, *ch 5, sk next ch-5 sp, sc in next ch-4 sp, ch 4, sc in next ch-4 sp, ch 5, sk next ch-5 sp, shell in ch sp of next shell, ch 3, sk next ch-3 sp, 2 tr in each of next 7 tr, ch 3, sk next ch-3 sp**, shell in ch sp next shell, rep from * around, ending last rep at **, join in 4th ch of beg ch-4.

Rnd 23: Sl st in each of next 2 tr and in next ch-3 sp, beg shell in same sp, *ch 5, sk next ch-5 sp, sc in next ch-4 sp, ch 5, sk next ch-5 sp, shell in ch sp of next shell, ch 3, sk next ch-3 sp, tr in next tr, [ch 1, tr in next tr] 13 times, ch 3, sk next ch-3 sp**, shell in ch sp of next shell, rep from * around, ending last rep at **, join in 4th ch of beg ch-4.

Rnd 24: Sl st in each of next 2 tr and in next ch-3 sp, beg shell in same sp, *ch 5, sk next ch-5 sp, sc in next sc, ch 5, sk next ch-5 sp, shell in ch sp of next shell, ch 3, sk next ch-3 sp, tr in next tr, [ch 2, tr in next tr] 13 times, ch 3, sk next ch-3 sp**, shell in ch sp of next shell, rep from * around, ending last rep at **, join in 4th ch of beg ch-4.

Rnd 25: Sl st in each of next 2 tr and in next ch-3 sp, beg shell in same sp, *sk next 2 ch-5 sps, shell in ch sp of next shell, ch 3, sk next ch-3 sp, tr in next tr, [ch 2, tr in next tr] 13 times, ch 3, sk next ch-3 sp**, shell in next shell, rep from * around, ending last rep at **, join in 4th ch of beg ch-4.

Rnd 26: Sl st in each of next 2 tr and in next ch-3 sp, ch 3, 2 dc in same sp, *sm picot, 3 dc in next ch-3 sp, ch 5, sk next ch-3 sp, sc in next ch-2 sp, [ch 6, sl st in 4th ch from hook, ch 2, sc in next ch-2 sp] 12 times, ch 5, sk next ch-3 sp**, 3 dc in next ch-3 sp, rep from * around, ending last rep at **, join in 3rd ch of beg ch-3. Fasten off. ■

double-ended crochet

This intriguing technique uses a double-ended hook and 2 skeins of yarn creating a reversible fabric. It's a simple technique that is easy and fun.

Double-ended crochet or "cro-knitting" as some have called it, is a type of needlecraft all its own. Similar to crochet in that you use only one instrument, the difference is that there is a hook at each end of the needle-type tool. It is somewhat akin to knitting, though, since half of the process is completed when you pick up loops, but leave them on the needle/hook. The loops are then worked off in the opposite direction. By turning and working back the other way with another color, the reversible effect is created, with each side of the fabric having a distinctly different color pattern.

With the double-ended hook, you can produce a unique two-sided fabric unlike anything you can get from a regular crochet hook or a knitting needle. The look is totally different and totally reversible. When people look at what you've created, they'll be amazed!

The basic stitch pattern is usually worked with two colors, with the colors used alternately for every other row. Using two skeins of the same color will create a solid pattern, and other combinations can be made using a variety of colors. You can add increases and decreases for shaping. You can add eyelets, puff stitches, popcorns and even crossed stitches. The stitches can be tall or short, can be made from almost any type of yarn and can be worked similar to almost any regular crochet stitch. There is no limit to what your imagination can create using this single needle with a hook at both ends!

There are two basic techniques covered in this book—working through the vertical bars and working through the horizontal bars. Working through the vertical bars, which is similar to afghan stitch, produces a thick, spongy fabric like a knitted garter stitch. Working through the horizontal bars elongates the stitches and spreads the rows apart, giving the fabric a softer feel yet keeping the ridged garter-stitch effect. Once you've mastered these two basic stitch patterns, the sky's the limit.

Double-ended hooks come in a variety of sizes, most commonly D through P, and are available as double-ended straight hooks and with a cable.

Shown here, you can see 3 gauge samples, all using same pattern, and 3 different hook sizes. The same stitch pattern takes on a different texture and look in proportion to the size of the hook used.

CROCHENIT HOOK

DOUBLE-ENDED SIZE G HOOK

DOUBLE-ENDED SIZE H HOOK

BASIC TECHNIQUES

Insert hook in 2nd chain from hook, yarn over and through *(see Photo A)*, leaving loop on hook.

Holding the double-end hook like a knife makes it easier to use.

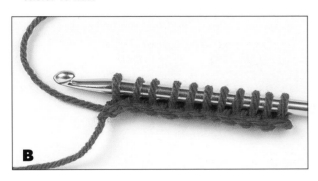

*To **pull up loop**, insert hook in next chain, yarn over and pull through, repeat from * across *(see Photo B)*, leaving all loops on hook,

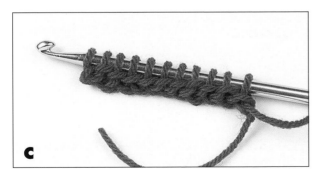

Drop color A, turn hook and slide all loops to opposite end of hook *(see Photo C)*.

*Note: Each of these loops counts as a stitch and is referred to as a **vertical bar**.*

To **work loops off hook**, with color B, place slip knot on hook *(see Photo D)*.

Pull slip knot through first loop on hook *(see Photo E)*.

Pulling the slip knot through first loop makes the first stitch of the row.

Yarn over, pull through next 2 loops on hook *(see Photo F)*.

*Note: When you pull through the 2 loops in this step, you will go through 1 loop of each color. The stitches you are making in this step are referred to as **horizontal bars**.*

G

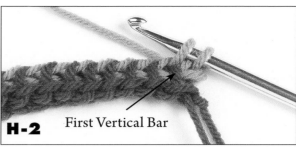

H-2 First Vertical Bar

To **work remaining loops off hook**, [yarn over, pull through next 2 loops on hook] across, leaving last loop on hook *(see Photo G)*, **do not turn.**

Note: You will now have only 1 loop on your hook. This loop counts as the first vertical bar of the next row. Never turn after working the loops off your hook.

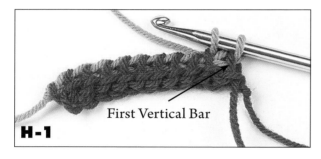

H-1 First Vertical Bar

TO WORK IN VERTICAL BARS
Skip first **vertical bar**, insert hook under next vertical bar, yarn over and pull up loop *(see Photo H-1).*

I-1

Pull up a loop in each vertical bar across, drop color B *(see Photo I-1).*

OR

TO WORK IN HORIZONTAL BARS
Chain 1, skip first vertical bar insert hook under top loop of next **horizontal bar** *(see Photo H-2)* between vertical bars, yarn over and pull up loop.

I-2

Pull up loop under top loop of each horizontal bar across *(see Photo I-2).*

Note: If you have trouble with your loops falling off the hook, cap the unused end with a rubber knit stopper or a piece of cork.

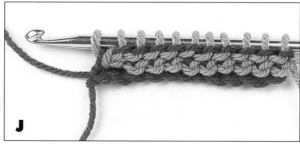

J

CONTINUE FOR BOTH STITCHES
Turn and slide all loops to opposite end of hook *(see Photo J).*

Note: To keep your yarn from tangling when you turn, rotate your hook back and forth rather than in a circle.

K

Pick up color A from row below, yarn over and pull through first loop on hook (*see Photo K*).

Note: This is the same process as in Photo E, except you are using the yarn from the row below rather than placing a slip knot on hook.

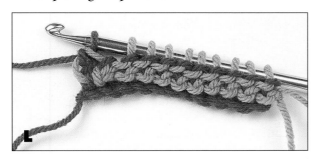

L

Yarn over, pull through next 2 loops on hook (*see Photo L*).

Note: Remember to go through 1 loop of each color when working the loops off in this step.

M

To **work remaining loops off hook**, [yarn over and pull through next 2 loops on hook] across, leaving last loop on hook, **do not turn** (*see Photo M*).

Continue alternating colors until ending with color A or color specified in individual pattern instructions. ∎

CROCHENIT TIPS

The Crochenit hook comes in 1 size only.

Use the red and green stoppers to help you keep track of when to turn your hook and which end of the hook you work with on any row.

As you turn your hook each time, remove the stopper and place in on the opposite end of the hook.

Before you lay your work aside, work until you have loops on the hook. Turn hook, place the green stopper on the end of the hook with which you will begin next time and place the red stopper on the other end.

Red means "Stop" and green means "Go"!

When you pick your work up again, you can start right away without having to figure out which end is the beginning. The stoppers also keep your work from sliding off your hook.

Even if you normally crochet holding your hook like a fork or a pencil, hold the Crochenit hook like a knife as you learn. This makes your work go much faster and easier.

For your first swatches in Crochenit, use two contrasting colors of yarn so you can clearly see your rows and stitches. As you become more experienced, experiment with two balls of the same yarn in the same color as well as yarns in different textures and weights. Just make sure the yarns you choose have the same cleaning requirements.

To keep yarn from tangling as you work with two balls of yarn, place 1 ball on each side of you. The first time you turn your hook, turn it counterclockwise. Next time, turn clockwise. Repeat. ∎

double-ended crochet
scuffs

DESIGN BY **DARLA FANTON**

SKILL LEVEL

INTERMEDIATE

FINISHED SIZES

Instructions given fit 9-inch sole *(small)*; changes for 9½-inch sole *(medium)* and 10-inch sole *(large)* are in [ ].

MATERIALS
- Medium (worsted) weight yarn: 2½ [2½, 3] oz/125 [125, 150] yds/71 [71, 85]g each raspberry and white
- Size K/10½/6.5mm double-ended hook or size needed to obtain gauge
- Size H/8/5mm crochet hook
- Tapestry needle
- Size 7–13 men's foam insoles

GAUGE

Size K hook: 9 sts = 2 inches; 6 pattern rows = 1 inch

PATTERN NOTES

Use size K hook unless otherwise stated.

Read Double-Ended Crochet on page 19 before beginning pattern.

INSTRUCTIONS

SLIPPER
MAKE 2.
UPPER

Row 1: With raspberry, ch 64 [70, 70], pull up lp in 2nd ch from hook, pull up lp in each ch across, turn. *(64) [70, 70] lps on hook)*

Row 2: With white, work lps off hook, do not turn.

Row 3: Ch 1, pull up lp in top strand of each of first 26 [29, 29] horizontal bars, sk next horizontal bar, pull up lp in top strand of each of next 8 horizontal bars, sk next horizontal bar, pull up lp in top strand of each of last 27 [30, 30] horizontal bars. *(62 [68, 68] lps on hook)*

Row 4: With raspberry, work lps off hook, do not turn.

Row 5: Ch 1, pull up lp in top strand of each of first 25 [28, 28] horizontal bars, sk next horizontal bar, pull up lp in top strand of each of next 8 horizontal bars, sk next horizontal bar, pull up lp in top strand of each of last 26 [29, 29] horizontal bars, turn. *(60 [66, 66] lps on hook)*

Row 6: Rep row 2.

Row 7: Sk first horizontal bar, pull up lp in top strand of each of next 23 [26, 26] horizontal bars, sk next horizontal bar, pull up lp in top strand of each of next 8 horizontal bars, sk next horizontal bar, pull up lp in top strand of each of next 24 [27, 27] horizontal bars leaving last horizontal bar unworked, turn. *(56 [62, 62] lps on hook)*

Row 8: Rep row 4.

Row 9: Sk first horizontal bar, pull up lp in top strand of each of next 21 [24, 24] horizontal bars, sk next horizontal bar, pull up lp in top strand of each of next 8 horizontal bars, sk next horizontal bar, pull up lp in top strand of each of next 22 [25, 25] horizontal bars leaving last horizontal bar unworked, turn. *(52 [58, 58] lps on hook)*

Row 10: Rep row 2.

Row 11: Sk first horizontal bar, pull up lp in top strand of each of next 19 [22, 22] horizontal bars, sk next horizontal bar, pull up lp in top strand of each of next 8 horizontal bars, sk next horizontal bar, pull up lp in top strand of each

of next 20 [23, 23] horizontal bars leaving last horizontal bar unworked, turn. (48 [54, 54] lps on hook)

Row 12: Rep row 4.

Row 13: Sk first horizontal bar, pull up lp in top strand of each of next 17 [20, 20] horizontal bars, sk next horizontal bar, pull up lp in top strand of each of next 8 horizontal bars, sk next horizontal bar, pull up lp in top strand of each of next 18 [21, 21] horizontal bars leaving last horizontal bar unworked, turn. (44 [50, 50] lps on hook)

Row 14: Rep row 2.

Row 15: Sk first horizontal bar, pull up lp in top strand of each of next 15 [18, 18] horizontal bars, sk next horizontal bar, [pull up lp in top strand of each of next 2 horizontal bars, sk next horizontal bar] 3 times, pull up lp in top strand of each of next 16 [19, 19] horizontal bars leaving last horizontal bar unworked, turn. *(38 [44, 44] lps on hook)*

Row 16: Rep row 4.

Row 17: Ch 1, pull up lp in top strand of each of first 14 [17, 17] horizontal bars, sk next horizontal bar, pull up lp in top strand of next horizontal bar, sk next horizontal bar, pull up lp in top strand of each of next 2 horizontal bars, sk next horizontal bar, pull up lp in top strand of next horizontal bar, sk next horizontal bar, pull up lp in top strand of each of last 15 [18, 18] horizontal bars, turn. *(34 [40, 40] lps on hook)*

Row 18: Rep row 2.

Row 19: Sk first horizontal bar, pull up lp in top strand of each of next 12 [15, 15] horizontal bars, sk next horizontal bar, pull up lp in top strand of next horizontal bar, sk next 2 horizontal bars, pull up lp in top strand of next horizontal bar, sk next horizontal bar, pull up lp in top strand of each of next 13 [16, 16] horizontal bars leaving last horizontal bar unworked, turn. *(28 [34, 34] lps on hook)*

Row 20: Rep row 4. Leaving long end for sewing, fasten off.

For center top seam, fold last row in half, matching sts, sew tog.

EDGING
With size H hook and raspberry, working in ends of rows, evenly spacing sts so piece lays flat, join with sc in first row, sc across. Fasten off.

SOLE
MAKE 2.
Row 1: With raspberry, ch 8, pull up lp in 2nd ch from hook, pull up lp in each ch across, turn. *(8 lps on hook)*

Row 2: With white, work lps off hook, do not turn.

Row 3: Pull up lp in first vertical bar, pull up lp in top strand of each horizontal bar across, pull up lp in last vertical bar, turn. *(10 lps on hook)*

Row 4: With raspberry, work lps off hook, do not turn.

Row 5: Rep row 3. *(12 lps on hook)*

Rows 6–9: Rep rows 2–5. *(16 lps on hook at end of last row)*

Row 10: With white, work lps off hook, do not turn.

Row 11: Ch 1, pull up lp in top strand of each horizontal bar across, turn.

Row 12: With raspberry, work lps off hook, do not turn.

Row 13: Rep row 11.

Rows 14–40: [Rep rows 10–13 consecutively] 7 times, ending last rep with row 12.

Row 41: Sk first horizontal bar, pull up lp in top strand of each horizontal bar across leaving last horizontal bar unworked, turn. *(14 lps on hook)*

Row 42: Rep row 10.

Row 43: Rep row 41. *(12 lps on hook)*

Rows 44 & 45: Rep rows 12 and 11.

SMALL SIZE ONLY
Rows 46–48: Rep rows 10–12.

MEDIUM & LARGE SIZES ONLY
Rows [46–52, 46–56]: [Rep rows 10–13 consecutively] [2, 3] times, ending last rep with row 12.

ALL SIZES
Row 49 [53, 57]: Rep row 41. *(10 lps on hook)*

Row 50 [54, 58]: Rep row 10.

Row 51 [55, 59]: Rep row 41. *(8 lps on hook)*

Row 52 [56, 60]: Rep row 12.

Row 53 [57, 61]: Ch 1, sl st in top strand of each horizontal bar across. Fasten off.

FINISHING

1. Rounding edges, trim away 1½ [1½, 1½] inches from toe and 1 [½, 0] inch from heel end of foam insole.

2. Holding 2 Soles tog with foam insole between and predominantly white side at top, matching sts, with H hook and raspberry, sc tog.

3. Easing to fit, sew Upper to Sole. ■

double-ended crochet
picot-edged afghan

DESIGN BY **CAROLYN CHRISTMAS**

SKILL LEVEL

INTERMEDIATE

FINISHED SIZE
40 x 61 inches

MATERIALS
- Bulky (chunky) weight cotton yarn: 33 oz/1,054/936g green 21 oz/735 yds/595g white
- Crochenit hook

5 BULKY

GAUGE
Each Panel is 4 inches across

PATTERN NOTES
Read Double-Ended Crochet on page 19 and Crochenit Tips on page 23.

Join with slip stitch as indicated unless otherwise stated.

INSTRUCTIONS

AFGHAN
FIRST PANEL
Row 1: With green, ch 150, pull up lp in 2nd ch from hook, pull up lp in each ch across, turn. *(150 lps on hook)*

Row 2: With white, work lps off hook, do not turn.

Row 3: Sk first vertical bar, pull up lp in each vertical bar across, turn.

Row 4: With green, work lps off hook, do not turn.

Row 5: Sk first vertical bar, pull up lp in each vertical bar across, turn.

Row 6: With white, work lps off hook. Fasten off.

Row 7: Working in starting ch on opposite side of row 1, with loose ends of green on the right, pull up lp in each ch across, turn. *(150 lps on hook)*

Rows 8–12: Rep rows 2–6.

EDGING

Join white with sc in first horizontal bar *(see Illustration)* on row 6, *[ch 1, sk next horizontal bar, sc in next horizontal bar] across, 3 dc in end of next white row, ch 3, sl st in 3rd ch from hook, 3 dc in end of next white row*, sc in next horizontal bar, rep between *, join *(see Pattern Notes)* in beg sc. Fasten off.

Horizontal Bar

NEXT PANEL

Work same as First Panel.

EDGING

Join white with sc in first horizontal bar on row 6; joining to long edge of last Panel, [sl st in corresponding ch sp on other Panel, sk next horizontal bar on this Panel, sc in next horizontal bar] across, *3 dc in end of next white row, ch 3, sl st in 3rd ch from hook, 3 dc in end of next white row*, sc in next horizontal bar, [ch 1, sk next horizontal bar, sc in next horizontal bar] across, rep between *, join in beg sc. Fasten off.

Rep Next Panel 8 times for a total of 10 Panels. ■

felting

Felting is not a precise science. Wool felts when exposed to water, heat and agitation, but each element is hard to control precisely. As a result, each individual garment may vary in the way it felts. Be sure to use 100 percent wool for felting projects; washable wools will not felt.

THE FELT FORMULA

Felting can be done in a sink, but washing machines get the job done more quickly. Each washing machine is different, and the amount your machine felts a piece after one cycle may vary from your neighbor's, so be sure to follow the specific felting instructions of the piece you are making. Check your piece a few times during your felting process to make sure you are getting the desired results.

The felting process releases fibers which can clog your washing machine. Therefore, you may want to place items to be felted in a roomy mesh bag before putting them in the washing machine. Also, adding other laundry when felting will increase the amount of agitation and speed up the process. Be careful, though, to use items that won't shed fibers of their own (*such as jeans*).

FELTING FACTS

Felting a knit or crochet piece makes it shrink. Therefore, the piece you knit or crochet must start out much bigger than the finished felted size will be. How much will it shrink? Good question. Shrinkage varies since there are so many factors that affect it. These variables include water temperature, the hardness of the water, how much (*and how long*) the piece is agitated, the amount and type of soap used, yarn brand and color. You can control how much your piece felts by watching it closely. Check your piece after about 10 minutes to

BEFORE

AFTER

see how quickly it is felting. Look at the stitch definition and size to determine if the piece has been felted enough.

HOW TO FELT

Place items to be felted in the washing machine along with 1 tablespoon of detergent and a pair of jeans or other laundry. *(Remember, do not wash felting with other clothing that releases its own fibers.)* Set washing machine on smallest load using hot water. Start machine and check progress after 10 minutes. Check progress more frequently after piece starts to felt. Reset the machine if needed to continue the agitation cycle. As the piece becomes more felted, you may need to pull it into shape. When the piece has felted to the desired size, rinse it by hand in warm water.

Remove the excess water either by rolling in a towel and squeezing, or in the spin cycle of your washing machine.

Block the piece into shape and let air dry. For pieces that need to conform to a particular shape *(such as a hat or purse)*, it may be helpful to stuff the piece with a towel to help it hold its shape while drying. ■

felting

pretty pansy bag

DESIGN BY **JEWDY LAMBERT**

SKILL LEVEL

INTERMEDIATE

FINISHED SIZE

9 inches tall after felting

MATERIALS

- Medium (worsted) weight wool yarn:
  9 oz/450 yds/255g periwinkle
  5 oz/250 yds/142g each yellow-green, leaf green, yellow, rose and purple
- Size I/9/5.5mm crochet hook or size needed to obtain gauge
- Tapestry needle

4 MEDIUM

GAUGE

14 sts = 4 inches; 10 rows = 4 inches

PATTERN NOTES

Avoid superwash or machine-washable wools.

Join with slip stitch as indicated unless otherwise stated.

Chain-3 at beginning of row or round counts as first double crochet unless otherwise stated.

SPECIAL STITCH

Popcorn (pc): 7 tr as indicated in instructions, drop lp from hook, insert hook in first tr of group, pull dropped lp through, ch 1.

INSTRUCTIONS

BAG
FRONT BODY

Row 1: With periwinkle, ch 46, sc in 2nd ch from hook and in each ch across, turn. *(45 sc)*

Rows 2–20: Ch 1, sc in each st across, turn.

FRONT SHAPING

Row 1: Ch 1, sk first st, sc in each of next 10 sts, working in back lps *(see Stitch Guide)*, hdc in each of next 23 sts, sc in each of next 10 sts, leaving last st unworked, turn. *(43 sts)*

Row 2: Sk first st, sc in each of next 9 sts, working in back lps, hdc in each of next 23 sts, working in both lps, sc in each of next 9 sts, leaving last st unworked, turn. *(41 sts)*

Row 3: Sk first st, sc in each of next 8 sts, working in back lps, hdc in each of next 23 sts, working in both lps, sc in each of next 8 sts, leaving last st unworked, turn. *(39 sts)*

Row 4: Sk first st, sc in each of next 7 sts, working in back lps, hdc in each of next 23 sts, working in both lps, sc in each of next 7 sts, leaving last st unworked, turn. *(37 sts)*

Row 5: Sk first st, sc in each of next 6 sts, working in back lps, hdc in each of next 23 sts, working in both lps, sc in each of next 6 sts, leaving last st unworked, turn. *(35 sts)*

Row 6: Sk first st, sc in each of next 5 sts, working in back lps, hdc in each of next 23 sts, working in both lps, sc in each of next 5 sts, leaving last st unworked, turn. *(33 sts)*

Row 7: Sk first st, sc in each of next 4 sts, working in back lps, hdc in each of next 23 sts, working in both lps, sc in each of next 4 sts, leaving last st unworked, turn. *(31 sts)*

Row 8: Sk first st, sc in each of next 3 sts, working in back lps, hdc in each of next 23 sts, working in both lps, sc in each of next 3 sts, leaving last st unworked, turn. Fasten off. *(29 sts)*

BACK BODY

Row 1: With periwinkle, ch 46, sc in 2nd ch from hook and in each ch across, turn. *(45 sc)*

Rows 2–30: Ch 1, sc in each st across, turn.

BACK SHAPING

Work same as Front Shaping.

FLAP SHAPING

Row 1: Working in starting ch on opposite side of row 1 on Back Body, join periwinkle with sc in 2nd ch, sc in each of next 9 chs, hdc in each of next 23 sts, sc in each of next 10 chs, leaving last ch unworked, turn. *(43 sts)*

Rows 2–8: Rep rows 2–8 of Front Shaping.

INSERT & HANDLE

Row 1: With yellow-green, ch 12, sc in 2nd ch from hook and in each ch across, turn. *(11 sc)*

Row 2: Ch 1, sc in each st across, turn.

Next rows: Rep row 2 until piece measures 64 inches.

Last row: Fold in half, matching sts on last row with starting ch on opposite side of row 1, working through both thicknesses, sl st in each st across. Fasten off.

ASSEMBLY

With Insert and Handle seam at bottom, working through both thicknesses, sc Front to 1 edge of Insert and Handle.

Working on opposite side of Insert and Handle, sc Back to Insert and Handle, leaving Flap unworked.

Turn RS out.

PANSY
TOP PETAL

Rnd 1: With yellow, ch 4, sl st in first ch to form ring, sc in ring, ch 3, [sc in ring, ch 3] 3 times, pc (*see Special Stitch*) in ring, sc in ring, ch 3, join (*see Pattern Notes*) in beg sc. Fasten off.

Rnd 2: Join rose in first ch sp, ch 3 (*see Pattern Notes*), (4 dc, ch 2, sc) in same ch sp, (sc, ch 2, 4 dc, ch 2, sc) in each of next 2 ch sps, (sc, ch 3, 6 tr, ch 3, sc) in next ch sp, working behind pc, (sc, ch 3, 7 tr) in last ch sp, join in 3rd ch of beg ch-3. Fasten off.

BOTTOM PETALS

Rnd 1: With yellow, ch 4, sl st in first ch to form ring, sc in ring, ch 3, [sc in ring, ch 3] 4 times, join in beg sc. Fasten off.

Rnd 2: Join purple with sl st in any ch sp, ch 3, (8 dc, ch 2, sc) in same ch sp, (sc, ch 2, 8 dc, ch 2, sc) in each of next 2 ch-3 sps, (sc, ch 3, 12 tr, ch 3, sc) in next ch sp, (sc, ch 3, 12 tr, ch 3, sc) in last ch sp, (sc, ch 2) in same ch sp as beg ch-3, join in 3rd ch of beg ch-3.

Rnd 3: Ch 4 (*counts as first tr*), [2 tr in next st, tr in next st] 4 times, ch 3, sc in next ch-2 sp, *sc in next ch-2 sp, ch 3, [2 tr in next st, tr in next st] 4 times, ch 3, sc in next ch-2 sp, rep from * once, sc in next ch-3 sp, ch 3, [2 tr in next st, tr in next st] 6 times, ch 3, sc in each of next 2 ch-3 sps, ch 3, [2 tr in next st, tr in next st] 6 times, ch 3, sc in each of last 2 ch sps, join in joining sl st. Fasten off.

Sew Top Petals to center of Bottom Petals.

LEAF
MAKE 3.

Row 1: With leaf green, ch 12, working in back lp, sc in 2nd ch from hook and in each of next 9 chs, 5 sc in last ch, working on opposite side of ch in front lps (*see Stitch Guide*), sc in each of next 7 chs, leaving rem chs unworked, turn.

Row 2: Working in back lps, ch 1, sc in each of first 9 sts, 3 sc in next st, sc in each of next 8 sts, leaving rem sts unworked, turn.

Row 3: Working in back lps, ch 1, sc in each of first 9 sts, 3 sc in next st, sc in each of next 7 sts, leaving rem sts unworked, turn.

Row 4: Working in back lps, ch 1, sc in each of first 8 sts, 3 sc in next st, sc in each of next 7 sts, leaving rem sts unworked, turn.

Row 5: Working in back lps, ch 1, sc in each of first 8 sts, 3 sc in next st, sc in each of next 6 sts, leaving rem sts unworked, turn.

Row 6: Working in back lps, ch 1, sc in each of first 7 sts, 3 sc in next st, sc in each of next 6 sts, leaving rem sts unworked, turn.

Row 7: Working in back lps, ch 1, sc in each of first 7 sts, 3 sc in next st, sc in each of next 5 sts, leaving rem sts unworked, turn.

Row 8: Working in back lps, ch 1, sc in each of first 6 sts, 3 sc in next st, sc in each of next 5 sts, leaving rem sts unworked, turn.

Row 9: Working in back lps, ch 1, sc in each of first 8 sts, 2 sc in next st, leaving rem sts unworked. Fasten off.

FELTING

Set water temperature to hot and water level to low.

Use small amount of mild detergent.

Felt Bag and Leaves separately from the Flower since the rose and purple dyes may bleed.

Felting process can take 10 minutes to an hour, depending on the wool.

Spin excess water out and shape Bag with towel folded and inserted in center. Let dry completely.

Sew Pansy and Leaves to Flap as shown in photo. ∎

filet crochet

This technique consists of groups of filled or open blocks. You'll learn to read a chart and be able to create beautiful picture designs.

Filet crochet is a combination of chains, double crochets, single crochets, slip stitches, triple crochets and double triple crochets.

These stitches form a series of blocks, some open, some filled *(see Photo A)*. The blocks then form beautiful designs.

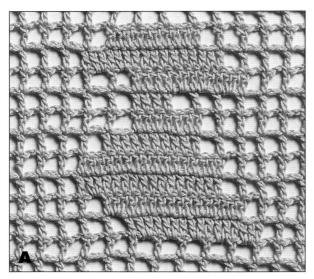

Most filet designs are worked from a chart of blocks or squares. On the charts, each vertical line represents one double crochet and each short horizontal line represents a chain-2. A block with a black dot is a filled block.

OPEN BLOCKS OR MESH

An open block or mesh is formed by a double crochet, a chain-2 and a double crochet *(see Photo B)*.

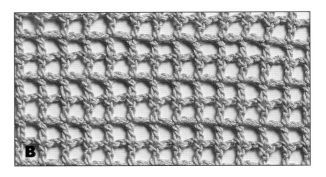

On the chart, a row of open blocks or mesh looks like this *(see Illustration 1)*:

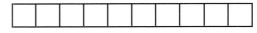

Illustration 1

It is worked as follows:

Dc in next st, ch 2, sk next 2 sts of previous row, dc in next st.

At the beginning of a row, the first double crochet and the first chain-2 of an open block or mesh is formed by a turning chain-5 that is made at the beg of the next row. At the end of a row, the last double crochet is worked into the 3rd chain of the turning chain-5.

FILLED BLOCKS OR BLOCKS

A filled block is formed by four double crochets *(see Photo C)*.

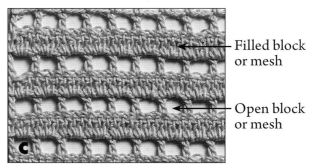

Filled block or mesh

Open block or mesh

If the filled block is over an open block, it is worked as follows:

Dc in next dc, 2 dc in next ch-2 sp of previous row, dc in next dc.

Note: *Double crochets can be worked into the chains of the chain-2 space, if desired.*

On this chart, a row of filled blocks is over a row of open blocks or mesh *(see Illustration 2).*

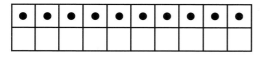

Illustration 2

If the filled block is over another filled block, it is worked as follows:

Dc in each dc *(see Photo D).*

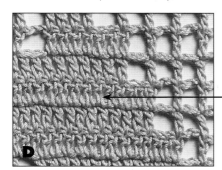

Filled blocks over filled blocks

On this chart, a row of filled blocks is over sanother row of filled blocks *(see Illustration 3).*

Illustration 3

On the charts, the last double crochet of 1 block is also the first double crochet of the following block.

SHAPING

Some of the projects are shaped by increasing and decreasing around the edges of the design.

On each chart the number of blocks for each row may increase or decrease *(see Illustration 4).*

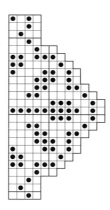

Illustration 4

INCREASES
OPEN BLOCKS OR MESHES

To increase one open block or mesh, work as follows:

A. At beginning of row:

Ch 8, dc in first dc of previous row *(see Illustration 5).*

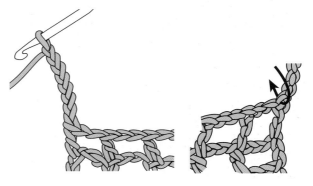

Illustration 5

Note: In subsequent rows, to work into a turning ch-8, dc in 6th ch of turning ch.

B. At end of row:

Ch 2, dtr in same ch as last dc made *(see Illustration 6).*

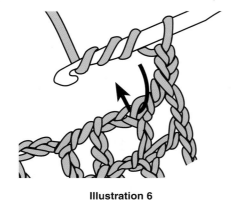

Illustration 6

To increase more than one open block:

A. At beginning of row, work as follows:

At the beg of the row, ch 8 for the first block and then 3 more chains for each additional block, dc in 9th ch from hook and then refer to chart to continue row.

B. At end of row, work as follows:

For first block, ch 2, dtr in same ch as last dc made, then work [ch 2, dtr in center of previous dtr *(see Illustration 7)*] for each additional block.

Illustration 7

CLOSED BLOCKS

To increase one closed block work as follows:

A. At beginning of row:

Ch 6, dc in 5th and 6th ch from hook and in first dc of previous row *(see Illustration 8).*

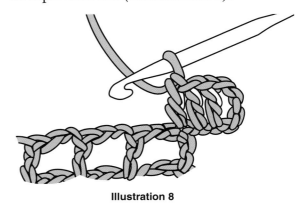

Illustration 8

B. At end of row:

Tr in same ch of turning ch as last dc made, tr in base of tr just made *(see Illustration 9)*, [tr in base of last tr made] twice.

Illustration 9

To increase more than one closed block:

A. At beginning of row, work as follows:

Ch 8 for the first block and then 3 more chains for each additional block, dc in 4th ch from hook, in each rem ch, and in first dc of previous row. Refer to chart to continue row.

B. At end of row, work as follows:

For first block, tr in same ch of turning ch as last dc made, tr in base of tr just made, [tr in base of last tr made] twice; then work [tr in base of previous tr] 3 times for each additional block.

DECREASES

A. When decrease is at beginning of row, work as follows:

At the beginning of the row, without chaining, sk first dc of previous row, sl st in each ch and in each dc to beginning of first block to be worked, ch 5, dc in next dc *(see Illustration 10)*.

Illustration 10

B. When decrease is at end of row, work as follows:

Work last charted block, turn, leaving remaining blocks unworked.

LACET STITCH

An additional stitch used on some charts is called a Lacet Stitch *(see Photo E)*.

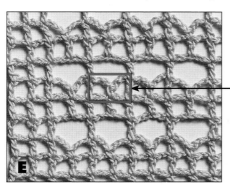

Lacet stitch

It takes the space of 2 blocks and is worked as follows:

Dc in next dc, ch 3, sk next 2 sts, sc in next dc, ch 3, sk next 2 sts, dc in next dc

On the charts, it is represented by a V-shaped curved line in a double-wide block *(see Illustration 11)*.

Illustration 11

To work over a lacet stitch, work bar as follows:

Dc in next dc, ch 5, dc in next dc.

On the charts, it looks like this *(see Illustration 12)*.

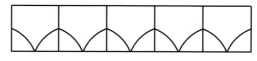

Illustration 12

WHEN WORKING FROM A CHART

When working from a chart remember that for each odd-numbered row which is the right side of work, you work the chart from right to left; but for each even-numbered row which is wrong side of work, you work the chart from left to right.

At times, designs will have charted half of the design. You will work the half of the chart to the center and then work the chart in reverse to complete each row.

To work the short rows at the ends of the charts, it may be necessary to finish off and rejoin the thread at various points. When rejoining thread, make sure to stay on the side necessary to continue the pattern.

Charts which have a design that is repeated have arrow symbols. These arrows denote the area which should be repeated for the desired length of the project.

To determine the number of chain stitches to be worked for the beginning chain of a design, count the number of blocks or mesh needed for the first row of the design. Multiply this number by 3. If the first block of the design is an open block or mesh, add 6 to the total and work the first double crochet into the 9th chain from the hook. If the first block of the design is a closed block, add 4 to the total and work the first double crochet into the 5th chain from hook.

For designs which have sections that are repeated for a desired length, additional chain stitches need to be included for each additional repeat.

JOINING NEW THREAD

Never tie or leave knots! In crochet, thread ends can be easily worked in and hidden because of the density of the stitches.

Always leave at least 4-inch ends when finishing off thread just used and when joining new thread.

If a flaw or a knot appears in the thread while you are working from a ball, cut out the imperfection and rejoin the thread.

Whenever possible, join new thread at the end of a row. To do this, work the last stitch with the old thread until 2 loops remain on the hook, then with the new thread, complete the stitch (*see Illustration 13*).

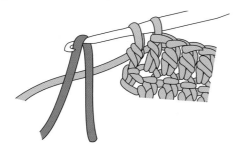

Illustration 13

To join new thread in the middle of a row, when about 12 inches of the old thread remains, work several more stitches with the old thread, working the stitches over the end of new thread (*see Illustration 14, shown in double crochet*). Then change yarns in stitch as previously explained.

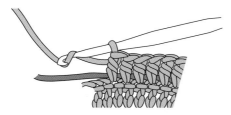

Illustration 14

Continuing with the new thread, work the following stitches over the old thread end.

WORKING AN EDGING

Although many filet pieces are stitched without an edging, you may want to add 1 to your piece.

A very simple but very neat edging is worked in single crochet and picots. This edging can be adapted to any filet piece by simply adding or subtracting repeats along each side.

PICOT

For a simple picot work as follows:

Work 3 sc as indicated in pattern, ch 3, sl st in last sc made (*see Illustration 15*).

Illustration 15

This makes 1 picot.

WEAVING IN ENDS

The first procedure of finishing is to securely weave in all thread ends. Thread a size 18 steel tapestry needle with thread, then weave either horizontally or vertically on the wrong side of work. First weave about 1 inch in 1 direction and then ½ inch in the reverse direction. Be sure thread doesn't show on right side of work. Cut off excess thread. Never weave in more than 1 thread end at a time.

BLOCKING

This means "setting" the finished project into its final size and shape.

Spread project out on a flat surface, having right side facing up. Dampen with water if piece has not been laundered.

Smooth project out to the correct size, having the design properly aligned. Use rustproof pins to hold the project in place.

To help retain the blocked dimensions, we suggest lightly spraying with spray starch. Let dry thoroughly. ■

indiana white daisies

DESIGN BY **JOYCE NORDSTROM**

SKILL LEVEL

INTERMEDIATE

FINISHED SIZE

52 x 76 inches

MATERIALS

- Size 3 crochet cotton:
  4,050 yds white
- Size E/4/3.5mm crochet hook or size needed
  to obtain gauge
- Tapestry needle

GAUGE

29 mesh = 9½ inches

PATTERN NOTES

Join with slip stitch as indicated unless
otherwise stated.

Chain-3 at beginning of row or round counts as
first double crochet unless otherwise stated.

Chain-4 at beginning of row or round counts
as first double crochet and chain-1 unless
otherwise stated.

SPECIAL STITCHES

Block: Dc in each of next 2 sts **or** dc in next ch-1
sp, dc in next dc.

Beginning mesh (beg mesh): Ch 4, dc in next dc.

Mesh: Ch 1, sk next st or ch sp, dc in next st.

INSTRUCTIONS

TABLECLOTH
PANEL A
MAKE 3.

Row 1 (RS): Ch 62, dc in 6th ch from hook (*beg
5 chs count as first mesh*), 28 mesh (*see Special
Stitches*), turn. (*29 mesh*)

Row 2: Beg mesh (*see Special Stitches*), 28
mesh, turn.

Row 3: Beg mesh, [mesh, block (*see Special
Stitches*)] 13 times, 2 mesh, turn.

Rows 4–8: Work according to Chart A.

STITCH KEY	
■	Block
□	Mesh

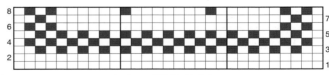

Indiana White Daisies
Chart A

Row 9: Beg mesh, mesh, block, 6 mesh, block,
ch 10, sk next dc, dc in next dc, block, 5 mesh,
block, ch 10, sk next dc, dc in next dc, block, 6
mesh, block, 2 mesh, turn.

Row 10: Beg mesh, block, mesh, block, 4 mesh,
block, ch 5, sc in next ch-10 sp, ch 5, sk next 2
dc, dc in next dc, block, 3 mesh, block, ch 5, sc
in next ch-10 sp, ch 5, sk next 2 dc, dc in next
dc, block, 4 mesh, [block, mesh] twice, turn.

Row 11: Beg mesh, mesh, block, 4 mesh, block,
ch 5, sc in next ch-5 sp, sc in next sc, sc in next
ch-5 sp, ch 5, sk next 2 dc, dc in next dc, block,

mesh, block, ch 5, sc in next ch-5 sp, sc in next sc, sc in next ch-5 sp, ch 5, sk next 2 dc, dc in next dc, block, 4 mesh, block, 2 mesh, turn.

Row 12: Beg mesh, block, mesh, block, 2 mesh, block, [ch 5, sc in next ch-5 sp, sc in each of next 3 sc, sc in next ch-5 sp, ch 5, sk next 2 dc, dc in next dc, block] twice, 2 mesh, [block, mesh] twice, turn.

Row 13: Beg mesh, mesh, block, 4 mesh, [2 dc in next ch-5 sp, ch 5, sk next sc, sc in each of next 3 sc, ch 5, sk next sc, 2 dc in next ch-5 sp, dc in next dc, mesh] twice, 3 mesh, block, 2 mesh, turn.

Row 14: Beg mesh, block, mesh, block, 4 mesh, 2 dc in next ch-5 sp, ch 5, sk next sc, sc in next sc, ch 5, sk next sc, 2 dc in next ch-5 sp, dc in next dc, mesh, block, mesh, 2 dc in next ch-5 sp, ch 5, sk next sc, sc in next sc, ch 5, sk next sc, 2 dc in next ch-5 sp, dc in next dc, 4 mesh, [block, mesh] twice, turn.

Row 15: Beg mesh, mesh, block, 6 mesh, 2 dc in next ch-5 sp, ch 1, 2 dc in next ch-5 sp, dc in next dc, 2 mesh, block, 2 mesh, 2 dc in next ch-5 sp, ch 1, 2 dc in next ch-5 sp, dc in next dc, 6 mesh, block, 2 mesh, turn.

Row 16: Beg mesh, block, mesh, block, 6 mesh, block, mesh, [2 block, mesh] twice, block, 6 mesh, [block, mesh] twice, turn.

Rows 17–23: Rep rows 9–15.

Row 24: Beg mesh, block, mesh, block, 6 mesh, block, 7 mesh, block, 6 mesh, [block, mesh] twice, turn.

Rows 25–41: Work according to Chart B.

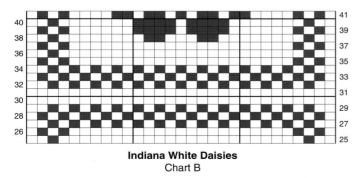

Indiana White Daisies
Chart B

Row 42: Beg mesh, mesh, block, 4 mesh, 4 blocks, 2 mesh, block, ch 10, sk next dc, dc in next dc, block, 2 mesh, 4 blocks, 4 mesh, block, 2 mesh, turn.

Row 43: Beg mesh, block, mesh, block, 3 mesh, 4 blocks, mesh, block, ch 5, sc in next ch-10 sp, ch 5, sk next 2 dc, dc in next dc, block, mesh, 4 blocks, 3 mesh, [block, mesh] twice, turn.

Row 44: Beg mesh, mesh, block, 5 mesh, 2 blocks, mesh, block, ch 5, sc in next ch-5 sp, sc in next sc, sc in next ch-5 sp, ch 5, sk next 2 dc, dc in next dc, block, mesh, 2 blocks, 5 mesh, block, 2 mesh, turn.

Row 45: Beg mesh, block, mesh, block, 6 mesh, block, ch 5, sc in next ch-5 sp, sc in each of next 3 sc, sc in next ch-5 sp, ch 5, sk next 2 dc, dc in next dc, block, 6 mesh, [block, mesh] twice, turn.

Row 46: Beg mesh, mesh, block, 5 mesh, 2 blocks, mesh, 2 dc in next ch-5 sp, ch 5, sk next sc, sc in each of next 3 sc, ch 5, sk next sc, 2 dc in next ch-5 sp, dc in next dc, mesh, 2 blocks, 5 mesh, block, 2 mesh, turn.

Row 47: Beg mesh, block, mesh, block, 3 mesh, 4 blocks, mesh, 2 dc in next ch-5 sp, ch 5, sk next sc, sc in next sc, ch 5, sk next sc, 2 dc in next ch-5 sp, dc in next dc, mesh, 4 blocks, 3 mesh, [block, mesh] twice, turn.

Row 48: Beg mesh, mesh, block, 4 mesh, 4 blocks, 2 mesh, 2 dc in next ch-5 sp, ch 1, 2 dc in next ch-5 sp, dc in next dc, 2 mesh, 4 blocks, 4 mesh, block, 2 mesh, turn.

Rows 49–59: Work according to Chart C.

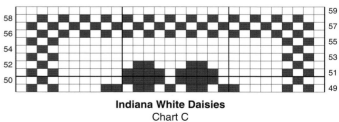

Indiana White Daisies
Chart C

Rows 60–175: [Rep rows 2–59 consecutively] twice.

Row 176: Beg mesh, 28 mesh. Fasten off.

PANEL B
MAKE 2.

Rows 1 & 2: Rep rows 1 and 2 of Panel A.

Rows 3–12: Work according to Chart D.

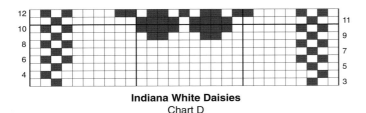

Indiana White Daisies
Chart D

Rows 13–19: Rep rows 42–48 of Panel A.

Row 20: Beg mesh, block, mesh, block, 4 mesh, 2 blocks, mesh, 2 blocks, mesh, block, mesh, 2 blocks, mesh, 2 blocks, 4 mesh, [block, mesh] twice, turn.

Rows 21–30: Work according to Chart E.

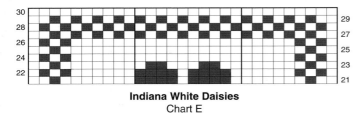

Indiana White Daisies
Chart E

Rows 31–146: [Rep rows 2–59 of Panel A consecutively] twice.

Rows 147–176: Rep rows 2–31 of Panel A. At end of last row, fasten off.

ASSEMBLY

Arrange Panels, alternating A and B. Hold first 2 Panels with WS tog and long edge at top, working through both Panels at same time, join cotton in end of first row at left-hand left end of Panels. Ch 1, work reverse sc *(see Illustration)* in same sp, working left to right, work [ch 2, reverse sc in next row] across edge. Fasten off. Join rem Panels in same manner.

BORDER

Rnd 1 (RS): With RS facing, join *(see Pattern Notes)* cotton in any ch-2 sp, ch 3 *(see Pattern Notes)*, dc in same sp, [2 dc in next sp] around, working (2 dc, ch 2, 2 dc) in each corner, join in 3rd ch of beg ch-3.

Rnd 2: Sl st in next ch-1 sp, ch 4 *(see Pattern Notes)*, sk next dc, [dc in next dc, ch 1, sk next st] around, working (dc, ch 4, dc) in each corner, join in 3rd ch of beg ch-4.

Rnd 3: Sl st in next ch-1 sp, ch 3 *(counts as a hdc and ch-1 sp)*, sk next dc, [hdc in next ch-1 sp, ch 1, sk next dc] around, working (hdc, ch 3, hdc) in each corner ch-4 sp, join in 2nd ch of beg ch-3.

Rnd 4: Sl st in next ch-1 sp, ch 4, sk next hdc, [dc in next ch-1 sp, ch 1, sk next hdc] around, working (dc, ch 4, dc) in each corner ch-3 sp, join in 3rd ch of beg ch-4.

Rnd 5: Sl st in next ch-1 sp, ch 3, dc in same sp, 2 dc in each rem ch-1 sp around, working (2 dc, ch 3, 2 dc) in each corner ch-4 sp, join in 3rd ch of beg ch-4.

Rnd 6: Ch 1, working left to right, reverse sc in same ch as joining, sk next 2 dc, [work reverse sc in next dc, ch 2, sk next 2 dc] around, join in beg reverse sc. Fasten off. ∎

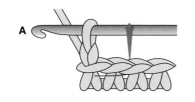
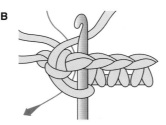
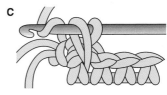

Reverse Single Crochet

It's simple and easy! Here are some great tips on how to cut fleece into strips for crocheting. You can join individual strips with a simple, no-sew method, or cut a continuous strip. Fleece strips can be crocheted just like regular yarn.

MATERIALS

The following materials are recommended for preparing your fleece fabric strips and crocheting them:

- Cutting mat
- Rotary cutter
- Size 13 tapestry needle (with large eye)
- Fabric glue, such as Beacon Fabri Tac
- Scissors
- Acrylic ruler
- Plastic crochet hook, such as Susan Bates Crystalites

GAUGE

Gauge will vary depending on the thickness of the fabric strips, size of crochet hook and pattern stitch that is used. Be sure to use the hook size that gives you the gauge specified with your pattern.

Fleece can be cut in individual strips or continuous strips.

INDIVIDUAL STRIPS

To make strips, make a template from a piece of cardboard in the size strips you need, clip across edge of fabric using template, and then tear or cut along the longest measurement of fabric piece.

JOINING INDIVIDUAL STRIPS WITH THE NO-SEW METHOD

1. Fold end over and snip to within ½ inch of edge, repeat on end of strip to be added (*see Photo A*).

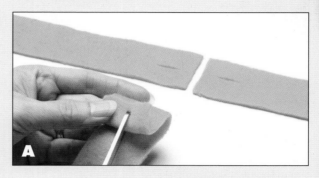

2. With right sides up, lap end of new strip over last strip, matching slits (*see Photo B*).

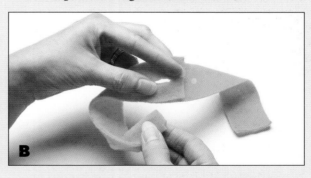

3. Pull other end of new strip through overlapped slits, bottom to top (*see Photo C*).

4. Pull strips until ends are hidden inside knot. Pull gently *(see Photo D)*.

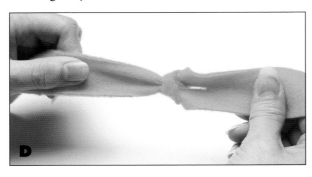

CUTTING CONTINUOUS FABRIC STRIPS

Lay fabric flat on cutting mat, folded lengthwise, with selvages together and folded edge toward you. Using rotary cutter and acrylic ruler, cut from fold toward selvages, stopping at the desired strip width from selvages *(see Illustration A)*.

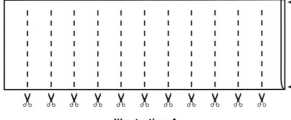

Illustration A

Referring to Illustration B, unfold fabric and cut through selvage at every other cut on one side. On other side, cut through the selvage at alternate cuts from first side.

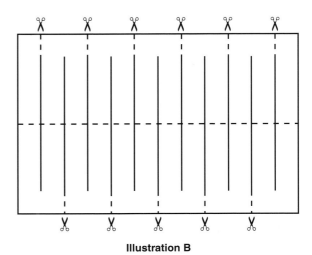

Illustration B

The thickness of the fleece will affect the weight of the finished yarn. Thinner fleece will approximate worsted weight yarn, while thick fleece will approximate bulky weight yarn. When cut into ½-inch or narrower strips the strip may roll in on itself while winding into a ball. Strips cut wider than ½ inch will remain flat.

HINT

You may choose to cut the corners where the fabric "turns" so that they don't stick out of the finished project as shown in Photo E. ■

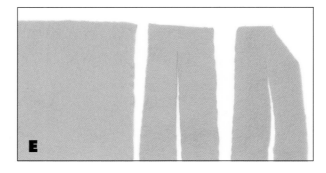

hats for all

DESIGN BY **SUE PENROD**

SKILL LEVEL

EASY

FINISHED SIZES
Instructions given fit baby, child and adult sizes, according to individual instructions and size of hook used

MATERIALS
Baby Version:
- Heavyweight fleece fabric:
  ¼ yd rainbow
- Size L/11/8mm hook or size needed to obtain gauge
- Tapestry needle
- Fabric glue

Child Version:
- Heavyweight fleece fabric:
  ¼ yd each raspberry and orange
- Size M/13/9mm hook or size needed to obtain gauge
- Tapestry needle
- Fabric glue

Adult Version:
- Heavyweight fleece fabric:
  ⅜ yd plaid
- Precut fabric strips:
  1 package off-white
- Size N/15/10mm hook or size needed to obtain gauge
- Tapestry needle
- Fabric glue

GAUGE
Size L hook: 10 sc = 4 inches

Size M hook: 9 sc = 4 inches

Size N hook: 8 sc = 4 inches

INSTRUCTIONS

BABY VERSION
Getting started: Cut fleece in continuous strip, ½ inch wide.

Row 1 (RS): With size L hook, ch 21, sl st in 2nd ch from hook and in each of next 3 chs, sc in each of next 16 chs, turn. *(20 sts)*

Row 2: Work rem rows in back lps *(see Stitch Guide)*, ch 1, sc in each of first 16 sc, sl st in each of last 4 sl sts, turn.

Row 3: Ch 1, sl st in each of first 4 sl sts, sc in each sc across, turn.

Rows 4–37: [Rep rows 2 and 3 alternately] 17 times.

Row 38: Fold piece in half with row 1 and row 37 tog, working through both thicknesses, sl st in each st across. Fasten off.

ASSEMBLY

Turn Hat RS out. With 16-inch piece of fleece and tapestry needle, weave fleece under 5th st from 1 end on every other row. Gather to close top of Hat. Tie ends in a bow.

Fold up bottom end of hat to form cuff.

CHILD VERSION

Getting started: Cut fleece in continuous strips, ½-inch wide.

Row 1 (RS): With size M hook and raspberry, ch 26 sl st in 2nd ch from hook and in each of next 3 chs, sc in each of next 21 chs, turn. *(25 sts)*

Row 2: Work rem rows in back lps *(see Stitch Guide)*, ch 1, sc in each of first 21 sc, sl st in each of last 4 sl sts, changing colors *(see Stitch Guide)* to orange in last st, turn. Fasten off raspberry.

Row 3: Ch 1, sl st in each of first 4 sl sts, sc in each sc across, turn.

Row 4: Ch 1, sc in each of first 21 sc, sl st in each of last 4 sl sts, changing to raspberry in last st, turn. Fasten off orange.

Row 5: Ch 1, sl st in each of first 4 sl sts, sc in each sc across, turn.

Rows 6–33: [Rep rows 2–5 consecutively] 7 times.

Rows 34 & 35: Rep rows 2 and 3.

Row 36: Fold piece in half with row 1 and row 36 tog, working through both thicknesses, sl st in each st across. Fasten off.

ASSEMBLY

Turn Hat RS out. With 16-inch piece of fleece and tapestry needle, weave fleece under 5th st from 1 end on every other row. Gather to close top of Hat. Tie ends in a bow.

Fold up bottom end of hat to form cuff.

ADULT VERSION

Getting started: For precut fleece strips, glue ends tog and roll in ball. For plaid fleece, cut continuous strip, ½ inch wide.

Row 1 (RS): With size N hook and plaid, ch 31, sl st in 2nd ch from hook and in each of next 3 chs, sc in each of next 26 chs, turn. *(30 sts)*

Row 2: Work rem rows in back lps *(see Stitch Guide)*, ch 1, sc in each of first 26 sc, sl st in each of last 4 sl sts, changing colors *(see Stitch Guide)* to off-white in last st, turn. Fasten off plaid.

Row 3: Ch 1, sl st in each of first 4 sl sts, sc in each sc across, turn.

Row 4: Ch 1, sc in each of first 26 sc, sl st in each of last 4 sl sts, changing to plaid, turn. Fasten off off-white.

Row 5: Ch 1, sl st in each of first 4 sl sts, sc in each sc across, turn.

Rows 6–45: [Rep rows 2–5 consecutively] 10 times.

Rows 46–48: Rep rows 2–4.

Row 49: Fold piece in half with row 1 and row 48 tog, working through both thicknesses, sl st in each st across. Fasten off.

ASSEMBLY

Turn Hat RS out. With 16-inch piece of fleece and tapestry needle, weave fleece under 5th st from 1 end on every other row. Gather to close top of Hat. Tie ends in a bow.

Fold up bottom end of hat to form cuff. ∎

mosaic crochet

Charted mosaic crochet is a wonderfully simple way to create elaborate and intricate-looking works of art. Without the bobbins, tangles and numerous yarn ends usually associated with color work, the technique is easily learned and requires little finishing.

HOW-TO

Only 3 basic stitches are used in mosaic crochet, the chain, the single crochet and the double crochet.

Mosaic patterns are shown to their best advantage when worked in highly contrasting colors. Alternate colorways have been provided for each project to illustrate how different color choices can dramatically alter the resulting fabric. Relatively rich, dark or bright colors paired with neutral tones usually yield the most striking results. Colors with a more subtle contrast can be used to create a completely different look from the same pattern. Begin by choosing 2 colors of worsted weight yarn and an appropriately sized hook.

Mosaic crochet is based on 2-row single crocheted stripes composed of a right-side row and the following wrong-side row in the same color. The color not in use is carried up the right-hand side of the piece. Color changes always occur during the last stitch of the 2nd row of each stripe.

To change colors: With first color, insert hook in last stitch, yarn over and pull a loop through. With 2 loops on hook, yarn over with the next color and pull through both loops. Do not fasten off, but leave the previous color at the right-side edge.

CHART READING

Mosaic charts are simply grids with white and color squares representing 2 yarn colors. Each mosaic pattern will assign a yarn color to these squares.

The first square of each row indicates the color to be used all across the row. Each square of the chart depicts 1 stitch or 1 skipped stitch.

Charts are read from bottom to top. Each horizontal row of the chart represents 2 rows of single crochet worked in the same color. The first of the 2 rows is a right-side (odd-numbered) row and is read from right to left. The following wrong-side (even-numbered) row is the same row read back across from left to right.

Every mosaic piece begins with a foundation of 2 rows of single crochet worked in color A. When color A is assigned to the white squares of the chart, these 2 rows are completed prior to beginning the chart. After completing the first foundation row, all chart rows begin with 1 chain stitch.

Chart 1 and Photo 1 illustrates the basic 2-row stripe in single crochet.

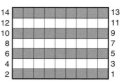

COLOR KEY
☐ Color A
▩ Color B

Chart 1

1

FOUNDATION

Row 1: With color A, ch 10, sc in 2nd ch from hook and in each ch across, turn. *(9 sc)*

Row 2: Ch 1, sc in each sc across, changing to color B in last st, turn.

BEGIN CHART

Row 1: With color B, ch 1, sc in each st across, turn.

Row 2: Ch 1, sc in each sc across, changing to color A in last st, turn.

Row 3: With color A, ch 1, sc in each sc across, turn.

Row 4: Ch 1, sc in each sc across, changing to color B in last st, turn.

Rep chart rows 1–4 for pattern.

Chart 2 shows a small mosaic pattern and Photo 2 the resulting fabric. Note that in Chart 2, there are both white squares on colored rows and colored squares on white rows. When squares of the opposite color appear on any given row, stitches corresponding to those squares are skipped. This is accomplished by chaining across the given number of stitches without working them. To prevent puckering or drawing in of the work, chain 1 more than the number of consecutive stitches to be skipped.

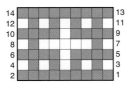

Chart 2

To skip 1 stitch, chain 2.

To skip 2 stitches, chain 3.

To skip 3 stitches, chain 4.

Skipping certain stitches leaves them free to be worked with the opposite color on the next right-side row. A double crochet stitch is used to reach down from the current row to the previous row of the same color

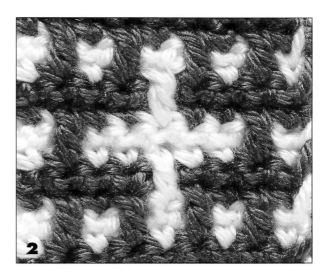

(see Illustration A). Within a mosaic pattern, all double crochets are worked in front of the chained spaces into the next stitch 3 rows below. Double crochets are used only on right-side rows. Wrong-side rows will consist only of single crochets and chains.

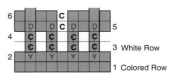

Illustration A

Compare the crocheted swatch to the chart as the written instructions are completed.

FOUNDATION

Row 1: With color A, ch 10, sc in 2nd ch from hook and in each ch across, turn. *(9 sc)*

Row 2: Ch 1, sc in each sc across, changing to color B in last st, turn.

BEGIN CHART

Row 1: With color B, ch 1, sc in each sc across, turn.

Row 2: Ch 1, sc in each sc across, changing to color A in last st, turn.

Row 3: With color A, ch 1, sc in first st, [ch 2, sk next st, sc in next st] 4 times, turn.

Wrong-side rows consist of working a single crochet in each stitch and a chain of the same length as was used on the previous row across the chain spaces thus:

Row 4: Ch 1, sc in first st, [ch 2, sk next ch sp, sc in next st] 4 times, turn.

Note that now there are 4 chain spaces on rows 3 and 4, leaving 4 open stitches on row 2. A glance at the chart reveals colored squares leading from row 5 across the previous "white" row down into the "colored" row before it. Every skipped stitch will now have a double crochet worked into it from 3 rows above.

Row 5: With color B, ch 1, [sc in next st, dc in sk st 3 rows below] twice, ch 2, sk next st, [dc in next sk st 3 rows below, sc in next st] twice, turn.

Row 6: Ch 1, sc in each of first 4 sts, ch 2, sc in each of next 4 sc, changing to color A, turn.

Row 7: With color A, ch 1, sc in first st, ch 2, sk next st, sc in each of next 2 sc, dc in next sk st 3 rows below, sc in each of next 2 sts, ch 2, sk next st, sc in last st, turn.

Row 8: Ch 1, sc in first st, ch 2, sk next ch sp, sc in each of next 5 sts, ch 2, sk next ch sp, sc in last st, changing to B, turn.

Row 9: With color B, ch 1, sc in first st, dc in next sk st 3 rows below, sc in each of next 2 sts, ch 2, sk next st, sc in each of next 2 sts, dc in next sk st 3 rows below, sc in last st, turn.

Row 10: Ch 1, sc in each next 4 sts, ch 2, sk next ch sp, sc in each of last 4 sts changing to color A, turn.

Row 11: With color A, [ch 1, sc in next st, ch 2, sk next st] twice, dc in next sk st 3 rows below, [ch 2, sk next st, sc in next st] twice, turn.

Row 12: Ch 1, sc in first st, ch 2, sk next ch sp, sc in next st, ch 2, sk next ch sp, sc in next st, [ch 2, sk next st, sc in next st] twice, changing to color B, turn.

Row 13: With color B, ch 1, sc in first st, dc in next sk st 3 rows below, sc in next st, dc in next sk st 3 rows below, sc in next st, [dc in next sk st 3 rows below, sc in next st] twice, turn.

Row 14: Ch 1, sc in each st across, changing to color A in last st, turn.

The chart is now complete. Note that the final 2 charted rows do not contain any chains. Since no rows will follow to fill in the skipped stitches, none are skipped. The last wrong-side row of the chart will always be a row of single crochet. Any rows not included in the chart are written out.

Row 15: With color A, ch 1, sc in each st across, turn.

Row 16: Ch 1, sc in each st across. Fasten off.

CHARTS WITH REPEATS

Chart 3 shows a mosaic pattern with a repeat. Note the vertical red lines separating the center section from the side stitches. The 7 stitches between the lines are the portion of the pattern to be repeated. The vertical lines replace the asterisk (*) used to indicate repeats in the written pattern. Horizontal lines will indicate where to end the pattern on the last repeat.

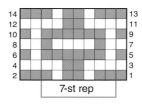

COLOR KEY
☐ Color A
▧ Color B

7-st rep

Chart 3

FOUNDATION

Row 1: With color A, ch 25, *(a multiple of 7 plus 3, plus 1 turning ch)*, sc in 2nd ch from hook and in each ch across, turn. *(24 sc)*

Row 2: Ch 1, sc in each sc across, changing to color B, turn.

BEGIN CHART

Row 1: With color B, ch 1, sc in first st, *[sc in each of next 2 sts, ch 2, sk next st] twice, sc in next st, rep from * across to last 2 sts, sc in each of last 2 sts, turn.

Row 2: Ch 1, sc in each of first 2 sts, *sc in next st, ch 2, sk next ch sp, sc in each of next 2 sts, ch 2, sk next ch sp, sc in each of next 2 sts, rep from * across to last st, sc in last st, changing to color A, turn.

Row 3: With color A, ch 1, sc in first st, *sc in each of next 2 sts, dc in next sk st 3 rows below, ch 3, sk next 2 sts, dc in next sk st 3 rows below, sc in next st, rep from * across to last 2 sts, sc in each of last 2 sts, turn.

Row 4: Ch 1, sc in each of first 2 sts, *sc in each of next 2 sts, ch 3, sk next ch sp, sc in each of next 3 sts, rep from * across to last st, sc in last st, changing to color B, turn.

Row 5: With color B, ch 1, sc in first st, *ch 2, sk next st, sc in each of next 6 sts, rep from * across to last 2 sts, ch 2, sk next st, sc in last st, turn.

Row 6: Ch 1, sc in first st, ch 2, sk next ch sp, *sc in each of next 6 sts, ch 2, sk next ch sp, rep from * across, ending with sc in last st, changing to color A, turn.

Row 7: With color A, ch 1, sc in first st, *dc in next sk st 3 rows below, ch 2, sk next st, sc in each of next 4 sts, ch 2, sk next st, rep from * across, ending with dc in last sk st 3 rows below, sc in last st, turn.

Row 8: Ch 1, sc in each of first 2 sts, *ch 2, sk next ch sp, sc in each of next 4 sts, ch 2, sk next ch sp, sc in next st, rep from * across, ending with sc in last st, changing to color B, turn.

Row 9: With color B, ch 1, sc in first st, *ch 2, sk next st, dc in next sk st 3 rows below, sc in each of next 4 sc, dc in next sk st 3 rows below, rep from * across, ending with ch 2, sk next st, sc in last st, turn.

Row 10: Ch 1, sc in first st, ch 2, sk next ch sp, *sc in each of next 6 sts, ch 2, sk next ch sp, rep from * across, ending with sc in last st, change to color A, turn.

Row 11: With color A, ch 1, sc in first st, *dc in next sk st 3 rows below, sc in each of next 2 sts, ch 3, sk next 2 sts, sc in each of next 2 sts, rep from * across, end with dc in last sk st 3 rows below, sc in last st, turn.

Row 12: Ch 1, sc in each of first 2 sts, *sc in each of next 2 sts, ch 3, sk next ch sp, sc in each of next 3 sts, rep from * across, ending with sc in last st, change to color B, turn.

Row 13: With color B, ch 1, sc in first st, *sc in each of next 2 sts, ch 2, sk next st, dc in each of next 2 sk sts 3 rows below, ch 2, sk next st, sc in next st, rep from * across, ending with sc in each of last 2 sts, turn.

Row 14: Ch 1, sc in each of first 2 sts, *sc in next st, ch 2, sk next ch sp, sc in each of next 2 sts, ch 2, sk next ch sp, sc in each of next 2 sts, ending with sc in last st, change to color A, turn.

Row 15: With color A, ch 1, sc in first st, *[sc in each of next 2 sts, dc in next sk st 3 rows below] twice, sc in next st, rep from * across, ending with sc in each of last 2 sts, turn.

Row 16: Ch 1, sc in each st across, turn.

Rep rows 1–16 for pattern.

TIP

To avoid the twisting together of the 2 working yarns, alternate directions each time work is turned.

SUMMARY

Read charts from bottom to top.

Right-side rows are read from right to left.

Wrong-side rows are read from left to right OR simply single crochet in each stitch and chain across each chain space.

Colored row: Any row of chart that begins and ends with a colored square.

White row: Any row of chart that begins and ends with a white square.

ON A COLORED ROW

Colored square with a white square directly beneath it: Single crochet (sc).

White square: Chain (ch) the number of consecutive squares, plus 1.

Colored square with a colored square directly beneath it: Double crochet (dc) in front of chain into the free stitch 3 rows below.

ON A WHITE ROW

White square with a colored square directly beneath it: Single crochet (sc).

Colored square: Chain (ch) the number of consecutive squares, plus 1.

White square with a white square directly beneath it: Double crochet (dc) in front of chain into the unworked stitch 3 rows below. ∎

mosaic crochet

mosaic scarf

DESIGN BY **MARGRET WILLSON**

SKILL LEVEL

INTERMEDIATE

FINISHED SIZE
6½ x 68 inches

MATERIALS
- Medium (worsted) weight cotton yarn:
  6 oz/300 yds/170g color A
  12 oz/600 yds/340g color B
- Size H/8/5mm crochet hook or size needed to obtain gauge
- Tapestry needle
- Size 35 broomstick lace pin or knitting needle

4 MEDIUM

GAUGE
15 sts = 4 inches; 19 rows = 4 inches

PATTERN NOTES
Read Mosaic Crochet introduction (page 48) before working.

To change colors: With first color, insert hook in last stitch, yarn over and pull a loop through.

With 2 loops on hook, yarn over with the next color and pull through both loops. Do not fasten off, but leave the previous color at the right-side edge.

When squares of the opposite color appear on any given row, stitches corresponding to those squares are skipped. This is accomplished by chaining across the given number of stitches without working them. To prevent puckering or drawing in of the work, chain 1 more than the number of consecutive stitches to be skipped.

To skip 1 stitch, chain 2.

To skip 2 stitches, chain 3.

To skip 3 stitches, chain 4.

Skipping certain stitches leaves the stitches free to be worked with the opposite color on the next right-side row. A double crochet stitch is used to reach down from the current row to the previous row of the same color (see Illustration).

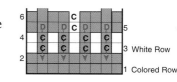

Within a mosaic pattern, all double crochets are worked in front of the chain spaces into the next stitch 3 rows below. Double crochets are used only on right-side rows. Wrong-side rows will consist only of single crochets and chains.

Colored row: Any row of chart that begins and ends with a colored square.

White row: Any row of chart that begins and ends with a white square.

ON A COLORED ROW
Colored square with a white square directly beneath it: Single crochet (sc).

White square: Chain (ch) the number of consecutive squares, plus 1.

Colored square with a colored square directly beneath it: Double crochet (dc) in front of chain into the free stitch 3 rows below.

ON A WHITE ROW
White square with a colored square directly beneath it: Single crochet (sc).

Colored square: Chain (ch) the number of consecutive squares, plus 1.

White square with a white square directly beneath it: Double crochet (dc) in front of chain into the unworked stitch 3 rows below.

SPECIAL STITCH

Loop stitch (lp st): Insert hook in next st, yo, pull lp through, wrap yarn from front to back around broomstick pin, knitting needle or 2 fingers, yo, complete as sc.

INSTRUCTIONS

SCARF
FOUNDATION

Row 1 (RS): With color A, ch 24, sc in 2nd ch from hook and in each ch across, turn. *(23 sc)*

Row 2: Ch 1, sc in each st across, changing to color B, turn.

CHART

Rows 3–10: Work rows 3–10 of chart.

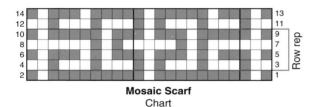

Mosaic Scarf
Chart

COLOR KEY
☐ Color A
▦ Color B

Rows 11–316: [Rep rows 3–10 consecutively] 38 times or to desired length.

Rows 317–320: Work rows 11–14 on chart.

Row 321: With color A, ch 1, sc in first st, dc in next sk st 3 rows below, sc in each of next 3 sts, [dc in next sk st 3 rows below, sc in each of next 5 sts] twice, dc in next sk st 3 rows below, sc in each of next 3 sts, dc in next sk st 3 rows below, sc in last st, turn.

Row 322: Ch 1, sc in each st across, turn. Fasten off.

BORDER

Rnd 1: Working around outer edge in end of rows and in sts, join color B with sc in lower right corner, 2 sc in same st, sc in each of next 2 rows, *[sk next row, sc in each of next 3 rows] across to corner, 3 sc in corner* sc in each st across top edge, 3 sc in next corner, sc in each of next 2 rows, rep between * once, sc in each st across, bottom edge, join with sl st in beg sc, turn.

Rnd 2: With WS facing, work lp st *(see Special Stitch)* in each st around, with 3 lp sts in each corner, join with sl st in beg lp st. Fasten off. ∎

hairpin lace

Hairpin lace is a decorative braid with a series of picotlike loops running along both edges. The loops are held in place by a rib which may be centered or offset. The rib is usually made of single crochet stitches but other stitches can be used for different effects.

The braid is made on a frame constructed of 2 or 3 parallel rods with the aid of a crochet hook.

Strips of braid may be used as they come off the frame as a trim. More often, strips are combined into larger pieces by looping or crocheting them together or combining with crochet.

Originally, hairpin lace was made from fine threads on a large hairpin (*the open kind used for attaching hairpieces*). For wider braids or braids with an offset rib, the lace maker might have used a dinner fork or meat fork for the frame. Today, commercial frames are used that are composed of 2 or 3 parallel rods held in position by a spacer at the bottom, and either

A

Photo A. Variety of hairpin frames. Left to right: ⅜-inch black enameled frame in form of hairpin without a spacer at the bottom, c. 1900; ¾-inch Boye frame, c. 1960; adjustable Susan Bates frame, c. 1970; adjustable Clover frame with 3 rods, 2003; 2-inch Boye frame, c. 1970.

a solid or removable spacer at the top. Some frames, especially older ones, are designed to produce only a single width of braid. Most modern frames are adjustable, so 1 frame will make a variety of widths. The Clover frame, with 3 rods, is needed to make hairpin lace with an offset rib.

YARNS & THREADS

Nearly any thread or yarn can be used to make hairpin lace. The key is to make the braid in a width that shows off your yarn to the best advantage. Here are some guidelines.

- Use fine, stiff threads for edgings on household linens. A thread with a tight twist, such as Aunt Lydia's Crochet Cotton, is ideal because the stiffness helps keep the loops in order and open.

- When using worsted weight yarn for afghans, keep the loops short so that the afghan doesn't become too open and lose its body. The afghan will be warmer, and no one likes his or her toes sticking through the fabric.

- Fuzzy and novelty yarns worked on a large frame show off the yarn to best advantage.

- Mix yarns with varying textures, weights and colors in alternating strips for more interest.

- Combine multiple threads for fringes.

GAUGE

A hairpin lace strip is stretchy. You cannot accurately measure the gauge of a hairpin strip.

For trims and fringes that use the braid as it comes from the frame, work as much braid as you think you will need and then stretch to fit. For a thin trim or fringe, work less. For a thicker trim or fringe, work more. A swatch can give you a guideline as to how much braid to make.

If a braid is finished with crochet, the crochet determines the gauge of the piece.

BRAID STRIP

Every hairpin lace project starts by making the braid strip(s). The strip is formed by wrapping yarn around one rod of a frame creating a

loop. Then the loop is locked into place by crocheting a stitch over the previous loop. There are many variations on how the yarn is wrapped and how the crochet stitch is formed. We have included instructions for the Basic Braid and several variations. For practice, we suggest you make a Basic Braid following the instructions below.

BASIC BRAID

The Basic Braid is formed by first wrapping yarn around a frame to form a loop. This is accomplished by turning the frame. Then the loop is locked into place with one single crochet stitch worked into the front of previous loop. These stitches form the rib of the braid. The width of the braid and the size of the loops are determined by the width of the frame you choose or as indicated in the pattern (see Photo B). The size of the rib is determined by the yarn size, hook size and stitch used.

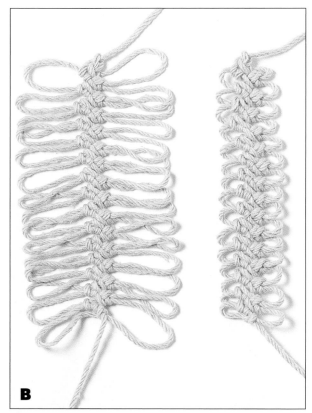

Photo B. Basic braids with loops of different sizes.

INSTRUCTIONS

BASIC BRAID

1. Position frame with spacer at bottom and rods 2½ inches apart. With yarn, make 1¼-inch loop with slip knot and place loop on left rod, having yarn end from skein in front of right rod. Bring yarn around right rod and across back of frame (see Illustration 1).

2. Insert hook through loop from bottom to top (see Illustration 2).

3. Hook yarn and pull through loop (see Illustration 3), ch 1 (see Illustration 4).

4. Drop loop from hook, with hook behind frame. Insert hook from back to front through loop just dropped, turn frame clockwise from right to left keeping yarn to back of frame (loop forms around rod), insert hook under front strand of left loop (see Illustration 5), yo, pull through, yo and pull through 2 loops on hook (see Illustration 6, single crochet completed).

Rep step 4 for desired length of braid (see Illustration 7). Fasten off by cutting yarn and pull end through last loop on hook.

Try to keep the first few single crochet stitches of the rib centered between the rods. After you complete several loops, the single crochet stitches will keep themselves centered.

Many projects require hairpin strips with more loops than can fit on the frame. When the frame becomes full, count the loops on 1 rod and mark each 10th, 25th or 50th loop with a marker, such as split-ring stitch markers or lengths of yarn. Slide the bottom spacer off of the frame and remove most of the loops. Add ribbon, thread or yarn to the bottom of each rod and slip loops onto them to keep loops in order. Put the spacer back in place and continue making loops.

When additional yarn is needed, add the new yarn along the outside edge of a rod by tying the 2 strands of the old and new yarns together. After strips have been assembled, simply weave the ends through the crochet stitches used to join the strips. On some patterns, you may need to add yarn while crocheting the rib section in order to hide the ends.

BASIC BRAID VARIATIONS

There are many variations you can make to the Basic Braid. These variations change the look of the rib and change the spacing of the loops. Like Basic Braid, all create a rib with a zigzag pattern.

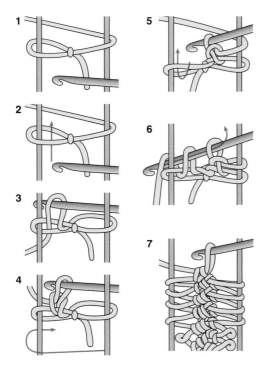

Hairpin Lace

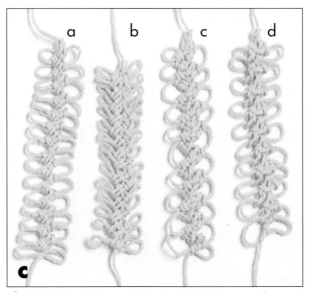

Photo C. Variations of basic braid: dc over front strand (a), basic sc over front and back strands (b), 2 sc over front strand (c), braid with sc over front strand (d).

BRAID WITH OTHER STITCHES OVER 1 OR BOTH STRANDS

Worked same as Basic Braid except with a double crochet over the front strand. Taller stitches, such as double crochet and triple crochet, space the loops farther apart. 2 or more different stitches can be worked over a strand such as a single crochet and double crochet (*see "a" in Photo C*).

BASIC BRAID WITH SINGLE CROCHET WORKED OVER FRONT & BACK STRANDS

Worked same as Basic Braid except single crochet over both front and back strands of previous loop (*see "b" in Photo C*).

BASIC BRAID WITH MULTIPLE SINGLE CROCHET OVER ONE OR BOTH STRANDS

Worked same as Basic Braid except with 2 single crochet stitches over the front strand (*see "c" in Photo C*).

BASIC BRAID WITH SINGLE CROCHET WORKED OVER FRONT STRAND

Basic Braid with single crochet worked over front strand (*see "d" in Photo C*).

BRAID WITH CROCHET BETWEEN LOOPS

Wide braids can be made by working crochet between instead of over the loops. A variety of crochet stitches or simple patterns can be used. For example, a braid with 5 single crochet stitches between the loops is shown in Photo D. To make a sample of this braid, follow the instructions at top right.

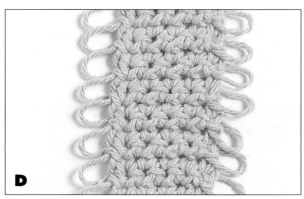

Photo D. A braid with 5 single crochet stitches between loops.

INSTRUCTIONS

SAMPLE BRAID

Row 1: Make loop with slip knot and place on left rod. Insert hook in loop from bottom to top, yo and pull through, ch 6, drop loop from hook, pass strand around right rod and across back, insert hook in loop in front of work.

Row 2: Sk first ch, sc in each of next 5 chs, ch 1, drop loop from hook, from back of frame insert hook in loop from back to front, turn frame clockwise.

Row 3: Sc in each of next 5 sc, ch 1, drop loop from hook, from back of frame insert hook in loop from back to front, turn frame clockwise.

Next rows: Rep row 3 for desired length.

BRAID FROM 2 YARNS 2-COLOR BRAID

Braids can also be made using 2 different colors of yarn (*see Photo E*). One yarn forms the loops which are wrapped around and around the frame without turning. The other yarn captures 1 or more strands as the rib is formed over the loops. The loops in these braids are not securely locked into place. A snag can distort a loop and its neighbors.

Any stitch that ends with a single centered loop can be used to form the rib in this type of braid. The simplest is a chain stitch. But stitches from the popcorn and cluster families can also be used.

CHAIN RIB

Example "a" in Photo E shows a chain rib over 1 strand.

Work as follows:
With first color yarn, make loop with slip knot and place loop over left rod. Wrap yarn around frame until desired number of loops are formed. With 2nd yarn, make loop with slip knot. Hold loop and yarn at back of frame. With hook, pull loop to front below first wrap, keeping yarn at back. Insert hook from front to back above one strand, yo and pull through loop on hook—ch st made, *insert hook above next strand, ch 1*, rep between * until all strands are used.

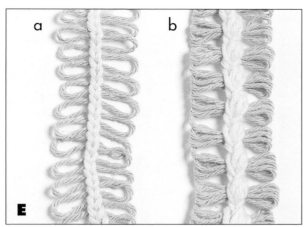

Photo E. Chain rib over single strand (a), cluster rib over groups of 3 loops (b).

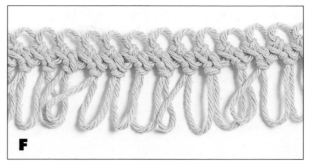

Photo F. Braid with offset rib.

CLUSTER RIB

Example "b" in Photo E uses a cluster over groups of 3 loops (*6 strands*).

Work as follows:
With first color yarn, make loop with slip knot and place loop over left rod. Wrap yarn around and around frame until desired number of loops are in place. With 2nd yarn, make loop with slip knot.

For first cluster: Hold loop and yarn at back of frame, with hook, pull loop to front below first wrap, keeping yarn at back, [insert hook from front to back above 3 loops (*6 strands*), yo, pull to front, insert hook below loops, yo] twice, insert hook above 3 loops, yo and pull through all loops on hook, working loops off 1 or 2 at a time if necessary (*cluster made*), ch 1.

Remaining loops: [Insert hook above 3 loops (*6 strands*), yo, insert hook in ch 1, yo, pull through ch] twice, insert hook above same 3 loops, yo and pull through all loops on hook (*cluster made*), ch 1.

BRAID WITH OFFSET RIB

Braid with an offset rib is ideal for trims and fringes although it can be used in larger projects too. This braid is made with a Clover frame that has 3 rods. Two of the rods are placed close together and the 3rd farther away.

Hold frame with narrow space to left and wide space to right.

INSTRUCTIONS

Hold frame with narrow space to left and wide space to right.

1. With yarn, make loop with slip knot and place loop over closest two rods of frame. Hold yarn at front. Wrap yarn counterclockwise around farthest rod and to back. In narrow space, pull up a loop under front strand, yo above strand, pull through (*first loop made*).

2. Drop loop from hook, from back of frame insert hook in loop from back to front, turn frame clockwise so yarn wraps around edge of frame with rods closest together (*2nd loop made*), in wide space, sc over front strand close to center rod.

3. Drop loop from hook, from back of frame insert hook in loop from back to front, turn frame clockwise so yarn wraps around edge of frame with rods farthest apart (*3rd loop made*), in narrow space, sc over front strand.

4. Rep steps 2 and 3 for desired length.

Many Basic Braid variations can be adapted to offset ribs such as working over both front and back strands, and using stitches other than single crochet.

DECORATIVE TREATMENTS FOR LOOPS

Unless making a fringe, braid strips are either joined to each other or the edges are finished. While joining or edging, the loops themselves can be manipulated into decorative patterns. They may be open, twisted, grouped or crossed.

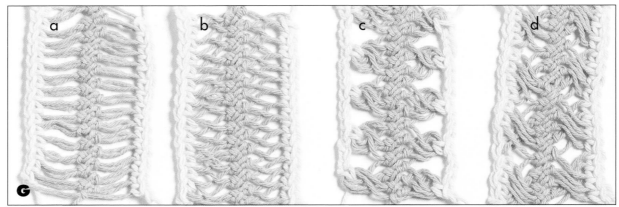

Photo G. From left: open loops (a), twisted loops (b), grouped loops (with twist) (c), crossed loops (open) (d).

These decorative loops can be used with any of the joinings or edge finishes described later. The examples here use a single crochet edge (*see Photo G*).

OPEN LOOPS

Enter loop from front to back, yo, pull through loop, yo and pull through 2 loops on hook (*sc made*). Rep along edge of braid.

TWISTED LOOPS

Insert hook from back to front, bring hook to normal crochet position, yo, pull through loop, yo and pull through 2 loops on hook (*sc made*). Rep along braid.

GROUPED LOOPS

Open or twisted loops may be grouped together in groups of any number of loops.

To group open loops together with an sc, insert hook through each loop from front to back, keeping each loop on hook, yo and pull through all but 2 loops on hook, yo and pull through 2 loops on hook (*sc made*). To keep braid flat, work 1, 2 or 3 chs between groups.

To group 3 twisted loops, as shown in Photo G, enter first loop from back to front, enter 2nd loop from back to front, enter 3rd loop from back to front, bring hook to normal crochet position, yo and pull through all 3 loops, yo and pull through 2 loops on hook (*sc made*). To keep braid flat, work 1, 2 or 3 chs between groups.

Loops may be grouped together with other stitches, such as double crochets or triple crochets.

To group 3 loops together with a dc, yo, insert hook in first loop, yo, pull through loop, yo and pull through 2 lps on hook, [yo, insert hook in next loop, yo, pull through loop, yo and pull through 2 lps on hook] twice, yo and pull through all 3 lps on hook (*dc made*).

CROSSED LOOPS

For 2-over-2 crossed loops with the loops worked open as shown in Photo G, sk 2 loops, enter 3rd loop from front to back, yo and pull through loop, yo and pull through 2 loops on hook (*sc made*), enter 4th loop from front to back, yo and pull through loop, yo and pull through 2 loops on hook (*sc made*), enter first skipped loop from front to back, yo and pull through loop, yo and pull through 2 loops on hook (*sc made*), enter 2nd skipped loop from front to back, yo and pull through loop, yo and pull through 2 loops on hook (*sc made*).

Rep with groups of 4 loops along edge of braid.

EDGES

Edges are used to stabilize and/or finish edges of braid strips. Edges may be made without adding yarn by chaining loops together, or they may be made by working crochet stitches through the loops.

LOOPED EDGE

Insert hook in first loop, *insert hook in next loop, pull loop through loop on hook*, rep

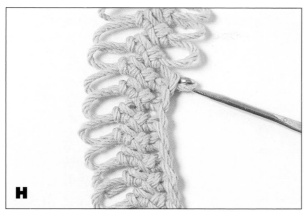

Photo H. Looped edge.

between * for desired length. Secure last loop by tying end of rib through loop.

SINGLE CROCHET EDGE

Single crochet is the simplest and fastest way to edge a braid strip. For braids with single crochet ribs, one single crochet stitch in each loop is used. For braids using taller stitches, like double crochet which spread the loops apart, or for grouped loops, single crochet stitches are spaced with chain stitches.

SINGLE CROCHET EDGE ON BRAID WITH SINGLE CROCHET RIB

Sc in each loop along edge.

SINGLE CROCHET EDGE ON BRAID WITH DOUBLE CROCHET RIB

Sc in loop, ch 1, rep between * along edge.

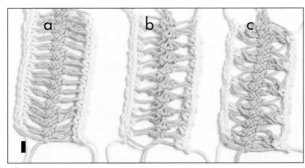

Photo I. Left to right: single crochet in each loop on braid with single crochet rib (a); (single crochet, chain 1) on braid with double crochet rib (b); (sc in 3 loops, chain 2 or 3) on braid with grouped loops (c).

SINGLE CROCHET EDGE ON GROUPED LOOPS

Sc dec (see Stitch Guide) in next 3 loops, ch 2 or ch 3 so that braid lies flat, rep between * along edge.

EDGES USING OTHER CROCHET STITCHES

Edges using double crochet and taller stitches make a more flexible braid than single crochet. The loops are not held as rigidly in place allowing the braid to flex more easily. This type of edge is often used in laces where the braid forms a serpentine shape. Combine this type of edge with a narrow rib which also makes a more flexible braid.

BRAID WITH DOUBLE CROCHET EDGE

Photo J shows a sample that combines double crochet and chain stitches.

Work as follows:
Dc in each of next 3 loops, ch 3, rep between * along edge.

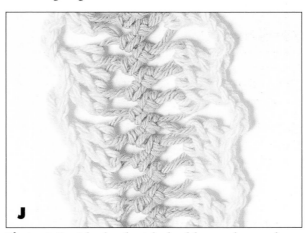

Photo J. Braid edged with double crochet and chain stitches.

JOININGS
BRAID JOININGS

Braid strips can be joined together to form larger pieces. Joinings are made with the loops. The 2 most common methods of joining strips are looping and crocheting.

LOOPED JOINING

A Looped Joining joins 2 strips of hairpin lace without using any additional yarn. The loops can be joined singly or in groups. The joining process can be done with either a crochet hook or the fingers depending on the size of loops.

LOOPED JOINING WITH SINGLE LOOPS

Lay 2 lengths of braid next to each other lining up loops, insert hook in first loop of right braid, insert hook in first loop of left braid, *pull loop of left braid through, insert hook in next loop of right braid, pull loop through, insert hook in next loop of left braid*, rep between * for length of braid, alternating left loop and right loop. Secure last loop by tying yarn end of rib through loop.

LOOPED JOINING USING GROUPS OF LOOPS

For groups of 2 loops as shown in Photo K, lay

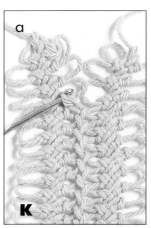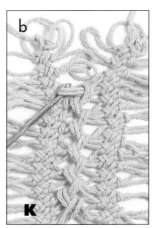

Photo K. Looped join (a). Looped join using groups of two loops (b).

2 lengths of braid next to each other lining up loops, insert hook in first 2 loops of right braid, insert hook in first 2 loops of left braid, *pull loops of left braid through, insert hook in next 2 loops of right braid, pull loops through, insert hook in next 2 loops of left braid*, rep between * for length of braid, alternating 2 left loops and 2 right loops. Secure last loop by tying yarn end of rib through loop.

SINGLE CROCHET JOINING

Single crochet can be used to join braid strips loop to loop or to join a braid strip to a crocheted piece (sometimes referred to as a crochet ground). In general, hold the 2 pieces to be joined with wrong sides together and single

crochet through corresponding loops of both pieces or through corresponding loop and stitch of both pieces. If the 2 pieces do not line

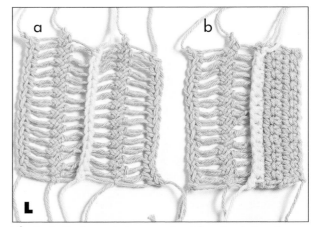

Photo L. Left to right: two braid strips joined loop to loop (a), braid strip joined to single crochet ground (b).

up stitch for stitch, work some single crochets through 1 side only or group some loops together to keep pieces even.

EDGED BRAIDS JOINED LOOP TO LOOP

Hold strips wrong sides together, matching loops, sc though 1 loop from front braid and 1 loop from back together at same time, rep for length of braid.

EDGED BRAID JOINED TO CROCHET PIECE

Hold strip and crochet piece with wrong sides together, matching loops with stitches in piece, sc 1 loop and 1 st of piece together at same time, rep for length of braid.

JOIN EDGED BRAIDS

Strips are often edged and then the edged strips joined. A row of single crochet for the first row of an edging gives maximum stability. Then more rows in various stitches can be added to provide a decorative effect. The additional rows of stitches typically use stitch combinations that are used as edgings on crochet such as a fan stitch edge or row(s) of double crochet. The edged braids are then joined just as crochet pieces are joined. The single crochet join and the chain mesh join are favorites.

CHAIN MESH JOINING FOR EDGED BRAIDS

The example in Photo M uses braid strips edged in single crochet.

Hold braid strips with wrong sides together, carefully matching loops, sl st in first sc in edge of front braid, sl st in 2nd sc on back braid, *sk next 2 sc in front braid, sl st in next sc, sk next 2 sc on back braid, sl st in next sc*, rep between * for length of braids.

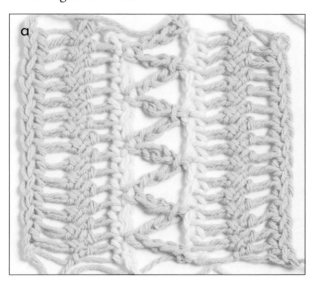

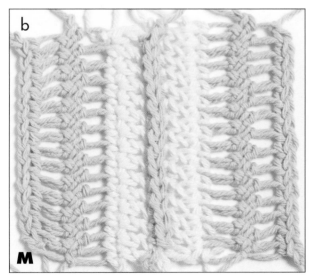

Photo M. Top to bottom: braid edged with single crochet and then strips joined with chain mesh (a), braid edged with a row of single crochet then a row of double crochet and joined with single crochet (b).

SINGLE CROCHET JOINING FOR EDGED BRAIDS

Example in Photo M uses braid strips edged in single crochet.

Hold braid strips with wrong sides together, carefully matching loops, sc through both lps of each sc of front and back braids together at same time, rep for length of braids.

RIB JOINING

A single braid strip may be joined to form a ring. To do this, join the ends of the rib using the yarn ends of the rib and a crochet hook or tapestry needle. Insert the ends through the rib completing the rib pattern as much as possible. Finish off on the wrong side.

ROSETTES

Braid strips can also be formed into circles or squares for use in motifs. The loops are gathered together on one side to form a center. The loops on the outer side are worked or in groups. Loops can be worked either open or twisted. The braid strip needs to be flexible to form a circle or square, so use a narrow rib such as single crochet, or chain and long loops.

CIRCLE ROSETTE WITH TIED CENTER & TWISTED LOOPS

Photo N uses 24 loops on each side of braid strip.

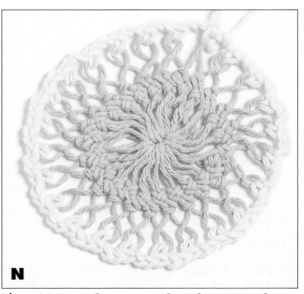

Photo N. Round rosette with tied center and twisted loops.

Before removing strip from frame, pass a 1-inch length of yarn through all loops on 1 side. Remove braid from frame. Tie ends of 1-inch length together so a small hole forms in center of rosette. Join rib using yarn tails of rib and a crochet hook or tapestry needle. Insert the tails through the rib completing the rib pattern as much as possible. Finish off on wrong side. Around outer edge, sc in each loop, inserting hook from back to front to twist loops. Make 2 chs between each sc. Join to form a ring.

SQUARE ROSETTE WITH SINGLE CROCHET EDGE FOR CENTER & OPEN LOOPS

Photo O uses 32 loops on each side of braid strip.

Along 1 edge of braid strip, [sc dec *(see Stitch Guide)* in next 4 loops] 8 times, inserting hook from front to back to keep loops open, join to form ring. Join rib using yarn tails of rib and a crochet hook or tapestry needle. Insert the tails through the rib completing the rib pattern as much as possible. Finish off on back. Working around outer edge, *tr dec *(see Stitch Guide)* in next 4 loops *(corner made)*, ch 5, [sc dec in next 2 loops, ch 5] twice*, rep between * around rosette. Join to form square. ■

Photo O. Square rosette with single crochet edge for center and open loops.

ribbon candy afghan

DESIGN BY **NANCY NEHRING**

SKILL LEVEL

INTERMEDIATE

FINISHED SIZE
44 x 47 inches

MATERIALS
- Medium (worsted) weight cotton yarn:
  36 oz/1,800 yds/1,020g white
  6 oz/300 yds/170g each lime, pink, orange, yellow, lavender and turquoise
- Sizes H/8/5mm and J/10/6mm crochet hooks or size needed to obtain gauge
- Clover tool set at 6 and 8, or 3-inch hairpin frame

4 MEDIUM

GAUGE
Size J hook: 19 sc = 8 inches

PATTERN NOTE
Read Hairpin Lace on page 55 before beginning.

INSTRUCTIONS

AFGHAN
CHAIN RIB BRAID STRIPS
MAKE 3 TURQUOISE & 2 EACH LIME, PINK, ORANGE, YELLOW & LAVENDER.
Cut 3 strands 15 yds long of each of other colors.

With 1 strand white and 1 strand 2nd color held tog, with H hook, make lp with slip knot and place lp over left rod. Wrap yarn around frame until desired number of lps are formed. With 2nd yarn, make lp with slip knot.

Hold lp and yarn at back of frame. With hook, pull lp to front below first wrap, keeping yarn

at back. Insert hook from front to back above 1 strand, yo and pull through lp on hook (ch made), *insert hook above next strand, ch 1*, rep between * until all strands are used and you have 175 lps on each side. End by pulling end of yarn used for ch st through last ch. Tie end to 2 yarns used to form lps.

EDGING
Work all lps open. Hold strip with 1 side of lps at top, hold first lp at right-hand edge open with right side of ch at base facing; with white and size J hook, make slip knot on hook, remove lp from hook and hold in back of open lp, insert hook in open lp from front to back, twist lp by bringing head of hook to right of lp around front and back to beg position with head of

hook pointing toward back of work, twist lp in same manner once more, insert hook in lp made by slip knot and draw through twisted lp.

Row 1: Ch 1, *insert hook in next open lp, twist twice, yo, pull lp through, yo and pull through 2 lps on hook, rep from * across, turn.

Row 2: Ch 1, sc in each st and beg ch-1. Fasten off.

Work Edging in same manner on other lp side.

ASSEMBLY

Arrange Braid Strips in following color sequence:

Turquoise, lavender, pink, yellow, orange, lime, turquoise, lime, orange, yellow, pink, lavender and turquoise.

To join braid strips, hold 2 Braid Strips with WS tog, with size J hook and white, make slip knot on hook, remove lp from hook and pass hook through first sc of both braids, pull lp through, working through both thicknesses at same time, [ch 1, sl st in next sc] across braid. Fasten off.

Join rem Braid Strips in same manner.

EDGING

Hold Afghan with 1 short end at top, join white with sl st in first st in upper right-hand corner, ch 1, *4 sc in next twisted lp, sk next rib, 4 sc in next twisted lp, sc in row 1 of white edge, sk next joining, sc in row 1 of next white edge, rep from * across. Fasten off.

Rep on rem short end. At end of Edging, do not fasten off.

BORDER

Working across next side, sc in each st to first sc of Edging, 3 sc in first sc of Edging, working across Edging, sc in each sc to last sc, 3 sc in last sc, working across next side, sc in each st to first sc of Edging, 3 sc in first sc, working across Edging, sc in each sc to last sc, 3 sc in last sc, join with sl st in beg sc. Fasten off.

FINISHING

Steam Afghan to relax yarn and reset twist in lps. Set iron on synthetic and maximum steam. Working in small areas, hold iron several inches above Afghan, stretching braid widthwise so twisted lps lie flat. Steam heavily and let cool. ∎

intarsia

This colorful technique is made simply by changing yarn colors.

GETTING STARTED

Once you have chosen your project and have the yarns, we suggest winding several 3–5-yard lengths of each color onto bobbins. Bobbins (*see Photo A*) are a handy notion that can be purchased for use in holding the small amounts of yarn for each color. Simply wind the yarn around the bobbins and you are ready to begin.

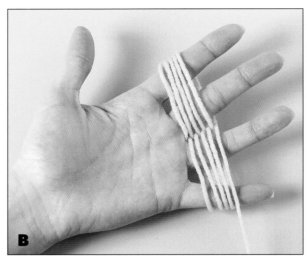

B

C

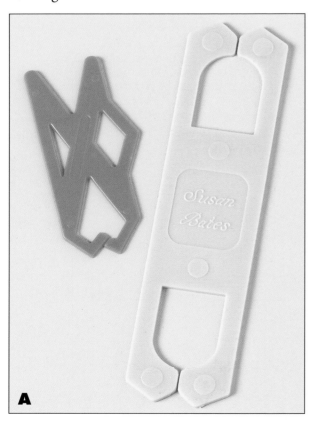

A

As an alternative, you may wind the lengths of yarns into figure-8 balls and pull from the center (*see Photos B and C*).

Or wind the yarns into small balls and place one ball of each color into a small zip-type plastic bag. Close the bag leaving a long strand for working (*see Photo D*).

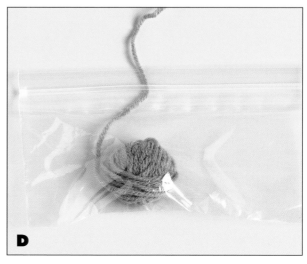

D

WORKING FROM CHARTS

Charts are easy to work from once you understand how to follow them. When working from a chart, remember that for each odd-numbered row, you work the chart from right to left, and for each even-numbered row, you work the chart from left to right.

Odd-numbered rows are worked on the right side of the piece and even-numbered rows are worked on the wrong side. To help follow across the row, you will find it helpful to place a ruler or sheet of paper directly below the row being worked.

CHANGING COLORS

To change from working color to a new color, work the last stitch to be done in working color until 2 loops remain on the hook (see Photo E).

E

F

Draw new color through the 2 loops on hook. Drop working color (see Photo F) and continue to work in the new color. This method can be used when change of color is at the end of a row or within the row.

CARRYING OR PICKING UP COLORS

To create some patterns, you may carry a color on the wrong side of the work for several stitches, or you may pick up a color used on the previous row. To carry a color means to carry the strand on the wrong side of the work. To prevent having loops of unworked yarn, it is helpful to work over the strand of the carried color. To do this, consider the strand a part of the stitch being worked into and simply insert the hook in the stitch and draw new color through (see Photo G). When changing from working color to a color that has been carried or used on the previous row, always bring this color under the working color. This is very important, as it prevents holes in your work.

G

WEAVING IN ENDS

Intarsia projects are worked with many color changes which result in many yarn ends. It is necessary to securely weave in all these yarn ends. Thread a size 16 tapestry needle with yarn end, and then weave running stitches either horizontally or vertically on the wrong size of the work. *Hint: Mark right side of work with a safety pin on first row for easy recognition of right and wrong sides.* First weave about 2 inches in one direction and then 1 inch in the reverse direction. Be sure yarn does not show on the right side of work. Cut off excess yarn. Never weave in more than 1 yarn end at a time. ∎

intarsia

sunshine tote

DESIGN BY **CAROL WILSON MANSFIELD**

SKILL LEVEL

INTERMEDIATE

FINISHED SIZE
11 x 13 inches

MATERIALS
- Medium (worsted) weight cotton yarn:
  7 oz/350 yds/198g burgundy

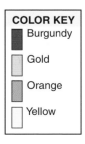

  3 oz/150 yds/85g gold
  2 oz/100 yds/57g each orange and yellow
- Size H/8/5mm crochet hook or size needed to obtain gauge
- Tapestry needle

GAUGE
4 dc = 1 inch

PATTERN NOTES
Please read Intarsia on page 68 before beginning.

Each square on chart equals 1 double crochet.

Chain-3 at beginning of row or round counts as first double crochet unless otherwise stated.

INSTRUCTIONS

TOTE FRONT/BACK MAKE 2.
Row 1 (RS): With burgundy, ch 50, dc in 4th ch from hook (*first 3 chs count as first dc*) and in each ch across, turn. (*48 dc*)

Sunshine Tote
Chart

COLOR KEY	
■	Burgundy
□	Gold
■	Orange
□	Yellow

(chart numbers: 1, 3, 5, 7, 9, 11, 13, 15, 17, 19, 21, 23)

Row 2: Ch 3 *(see Pattern Notes)*, dc in each dc and in 3rd ch of beg ch-3, turn.

Row 3: Ch 3, dc in each of next 21 dc, changing colors *(see Stitch Guide)* to gold in last dc, dc in each of next 4 dc, changing to burgundy in last dc, dc in each of next 21 dc and in 3rd ch of turning ch-3, turn.

Rows 4–24: Follow Chart.

At end of last row, fasten off.

FINISHING

1. Hold pieces with RS tog. Sew sides and bottom of pieces tog, leaving top edge open.

2. For braided strap, cut 6 strands each 3 yards in length of each burgundy, gold and orange. Using all the strands, braid to length of 45 inches leaving 10 inches at each end unbraided.

3. With burgundy, tack braid to each side seam of Tote leaving unbraided ends to form tassel at each corner and 23 inches unattached at top to form strap. ∎

slip-stitch

Slip-stitch crochet is the oldest crochet technique in print. It was first referred to in 1812 as shepherd's knitting in *The Memoirs of a Highland Lady* by Elizabeth Groves.

Typically slip-stitch crochet is worked through only 1 loop of the stitch in the row below. A stitch worked in the back loop *(see Illustration)* looks very different than a stitch worked in the front loop *(see Illustration)*, much like the difference between the look of a knit stitch and a purl stitch in knitting. Slip-stitch in back loops forms horizontal bars on the face of the fabric, and the fabric lies flat. Slip stitch in front loops forms vertical bars on the face of the fabric and has a pronounced curl toward the face of the fabric.

Back Loop   **Front Loop**

Slip-stitch crochet produces 3 distinctive styles of crochet—brocade, jacquard and ribbing. Brocade patterns emphasize the differences in look between working in the front loop and back loop to produce patterned fabrics. Jacquard patterns use one stitch throughout (it can be either front loop or back loop) but change color every few stitches to create a pattern. The 3rd use of slip-stitch crochet is to produce a very stretchy ribbing. The ribbing resembles 1 x 1 knitted ribbing in both appearance and elasticity, the main difference being that slip-stitch ribbing is worked at 90 degrees to knitted ribbing.

Slip-stitch crochet can be worked in either rows or in rounds. When working brocade or jacquard patterns in rows, the work is done in 1 direction only. The yarn is started and ended on each row. You may end up with a lot of yarn ends to work in if you don't want fringe. The reason that patterns are not worked back and forth in rows is that when you work slip-stitch crochet back and forth, a stretchy fabric is created, which is how slip-stitch ribbing is made.

Working in the round (in a spiral) allows you to work continuously in 1 direction without ends. You can work in the round as either a tube or a circle/oval. Tubes can be sealed at one end to make pouches or sealed at both ends to make a double-layered fabric.

When working in a tube, the beginning of each round migrates ½ stitch each round so that the beginning of each round spirals across the face of the work. For the purposes of the patterns in this book, each new round is considered to begin directly above the beginning of the previous round disregarding the migration of the stitch. Just line up the start of each round above the previous start and disregard the ½ stitch. ∎

brocade hot pad

DESIGN BY **NANCY NEHRING**

SKILL LEVEL

EASY

FINISHED SIZE
6½ x 7 inches

MATERIALS
- Aunt Lydia's Double Strand size 3 crochet cotton (300 yds per ball):
    1 ball #443 victory red/Mexicana
- Size E/4/3.5mm crochet hook or size needed to obtain gauge
- Stitch marker

GAUGE
15 sl sts = 2 inches; 10 sl st rows = 1 inch

PATTERN NOTES
Item is worked left-handed, checks will slant in opposite direction for right-handed crocheters.

Hot Pad is double-layered, worked as a tube.

Starting point will migrate ½ stitch to right on each round for right-handers and ½ stitch to left for left-handers.

Work in continuous rounds, do not turn or join unless otherwise stated.

Mark first stitch of round.

INSTRUCTIONS

HOT PAD
Rnd 1: Ch 51, sl st in front lp (*see Illustration on facing page*) of 2nd ch from hook and in each ch across, working on opposite side of ch, sl st in each ch across, do not join (*see Pattern Notes*).

Rnds 2–9: [Sl st in front lps of each of next 5 sts, sl st in back lps (*see Illustration on facing page*) of each of next 5 sts] around. At end of last rnd, sl st in back lp of each of next 5 sts. You will now start rnds here.

Next rnds: [Rep rnds 2–9 consecutively] 8 times.

Last rnd: Fold Hot Pad in half, ch 10 (*hanging lp*), sl st in same st, sl st in each ch around hanging lp, working through both thicknesses, sl st in each st across. Fasten off. ∎

slip-stitch
lap afghan

DESIGN BY **NANCY NEHRING**

SKILL LEVEL

EASY

FINISHED SIZE
40 x 55 inches

MATERIALS
- Medium (worsted) weight cotton yarn:
  42 oz/2,100 yds/1,191g linen
- Size N/13/9mm crochet hook or size needed to obtain gauge
- Stitch marker

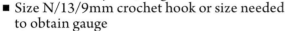

GAUGE
12 sl sts = 4 inches

PATTERN NOTES
Item is worked left-handed; diagonals will flow in opposite direction for right-handed crocheters.

Afghan is doubled-layered, worked as a tube.

Work in continuous rounds, do not turn or join rounds unless otherwise stated.

Mark first stitch of round.

INSTRUCTIONS

AFGHAN
Rnd 1: Ch 239, sl st in back lp *(see Illustration on page 72)* of first ch to form ring, working in back lps, sl st in each ch around, do not join *(see Pattern Notes)*. *(239 sl sts)*

Rnd 2: [Sl st in back lp of each of next 10 sts, sl st in front lps *(see Illustration on page 72)* in each of next 10 sts] 11 times, sl st in back lp of each of next 10 sts, sl st in front lp of each of last 9 sts.

Next rnds: Rep rnd 2 until piece measures 55 inches.

Last rnd: Sl st in back lp of each st around. Do not fasten off.

FINISHING
Fold tube in half, working through both thicknesses and in all lps, sl st in each st across. Fasten off.

Rep on opposite short end. ■

learn to crochet socks

Learn to custom-fit socks from the toe up. It's fun and easy once you get the hang of it!

HOW TO CUSTOM-FIT A BASIC CROCHETED TOE-UP SOCK WITH AN AFTERTHOUGHT HEEL

If this is your first time crocheting a sock, try using some nice, inexpensive worsted weight yarn. With thicker yarn, an average crocheter can complete at least 1 sock in 6 hours or less. Worsted weight yarn makes great slippers for around the house or sleeping. Start with 2 or more 50-gram balls and a hook at least 2 sizes smaller than the manufacturer's recommendation.

Working in a tight tension will improve the durability of your socks.

HERE ARE USEFUL TERMS:

Ankle—The joint where the foot meets the calf of the leg.

Arch—The curve on the bottom of the foot.

Ball of the foot—The area on the bottom of the foot between the toes and the arch.

Calf—The lower portion of the leg between the ankle and the knee.

Heel—The back part of the foot below and behind the ankle.

Instep—The top of the foot between the toes and the ankle.

GAUGE

The next step is the often-dreaded gauge swatch. Make the swatch in single crochets at least 5 inches square. In general, a bigger swatch will yield more accurate gauge measurements.

To measure the gauge, weave darning needles through the swatch 4 inches apart, but not too close to any of the edges.

A straight-edge ruler will yield a more accurate measurement than a tape measure. Set the ruler aside and count the single crochets in 1 row between the needles. Below is a work sheet to note your results:

1. With measuring tape, measure the circumference around the widest part of the instep of the foot (variable B). You may have thought you would never use the algebra they made you learn in high school, but, yes, you do need to use math when you crochet. A toe-up sock is just that—the work starts at the toe. Generally, adult socks start with a chain 2 inches long or 1-inch long for a child's sock.

2. Take the number of stitches in 4 inches (variable A) and divide that number by 2 for adults and 4 for children, add 1 for the turning chain (A/2+1).

3. Begin shaping the toe by working in both sides of the chain with 3 single crochets in the last stitch on each end of the chain, excluding the turning chain.

4. When the first round is complete, the number of single crochets should be twice the number of starting chains. Some sock patterns will give you stitch counts for each round of the toe.

5. Place a stitch marker in the center stitch on each end of the chain. Increase in the stitch before and after each marker.

6. Increase until there are enough stitches to go around the instep.

7. More algebra: Take the number of stitches in 4 inches (A in step 2), divide that number by 4 to get the number of stitches per inch (A/4). Multiply that number by the number of inches around the thickest part of the foot (A/4 x B) to get the number of stitches needed (variable C).

8. If you want to know the number of rows you will need, take the number of stitches for the circumference of the foot (C), subtract the number of stitches in 4 inches (A) and add 2.

Divide that number by 4 to get the number of rows of increases $[(C-A+2)/4]$.

9. Work the instep even to the ankle. If there is a significant difference between the circumference at the ball of the foot and the largest part of the foot, the sock will be a little baggy just above the toe. You may want to modify the pattern.

10. Measure the circumference at the ball of the foot (*variable D*). Subtract D from B $(B-D)$ and multiply the new number by the number of stitches per inch $[(B-D) \times A/4]$. This is the number of stitches you will need to increase between the toe and the ankle. Work the instep until it touches the front of the ankle or about 2 inches shorter than the length of the foot.

11. Work the instep even and be creative in the stitch combinations.

12. Crocheted fabric will bias when worked in continuous rounds. To prevent the bias, turn work at the end of each round. Work one round from the right side and the next from the wrong side.

13. An afterthought heel is worked last, after the ankle and cuff. Generally, the circumference of the largest part of the foot is about the same as the circumference of the ankle. To make a space for the heel, make a chain and skip half of the stitches around the instep.

14. Chain stitches do not stretch the same as other stitches. Use a slightly larger hook to make the chain or add a couple extra stitches to help the sock fit comfortably. Foundation stitches stretch very nicely. In a foundation stitch, you work the chain with each stitch.

15. Work a few rows of the ankle before trying on the sock. If the chain feels tight around the back of the heel, rip back to the instep and add a few more rows. If the toe is baggy, remove a few rows from the instep.

16. The ankle and the cuff are the place to let your creativity shine. You can work in continuous rounds or back and forth, joining with a slip stitch at the end of each round.

17. Crochet is not as resilient as knitting. For a higher cuff, work some elastic into the ribbing to help hold up the sock. Increase as necessary to fit over the calf.

18. Start the toe with the inside end of the yarn. Work part of the ankle. Use the outside end to work the heel. You can now use every inch of yarn that is left on the cuff.

19. Work the heel just like the toe, except in reverse. Join the yarn at one side of heel opening. Work single crochets around the heel opening. Place markers on each end so there are the same number of stitches on each side. Decrease before and after each marker until the stitch count is the same as the stitch count on round 1 of the toe. Turn sock inside out and whipstitch heel closed.

20. To prevent holes on each end of the heel opening, single crochet decrease in each end while working the first round of single crochets. If there are holes after working the heel, use the ends and a tapestry needle to make a couple stitches to close the holes.

21. Crochet does not stretch the same as knitting. It is also less resilient. Your sock should be a little snug. If it is too long, the heel will bunch up. The cuff will also sag if it is too loose. On the other hand, if the sock is too tight, you will have difficulty pulling it over the heel when you put it on.

22. The amount of yarn in a skein or ball is call its "put-up." The put-up for sock yarn is generally enough to knit 1 or 2 socks. Crochet uses 30 percent more yarn. If you want a longer cuff, buy extra yarn.

23. Toes and heels are the first places to wear out. For more durable socks, try working the toe and heel with two strands of yarn. The toe and afterthought heel are worked exactly the same but in opposite directions—1 with increases, the other with decreases.

24. For a hole in the heel, just frog it and add a new heel. If there is a hole in the toe, pick the stitches out until there is an even round. Work a round of single crochets through the bottom of each stitch. Work a top-down toe just like the heel.

FIBER CONTENT

The fiber content tells what the yarn is. Wool fibers have scales. They look like the damaged hair shown in shampoo advertisements. When wool is exposed to moisture, variable temperatures and agitation, those scales hook into each other like Velcro and cause the fabric to shrink and felt. Untreated wool should be hand-washed, rinsed in cool water and allowed to air dry.

But who wants to hand-wash socks? If you like wool but not hand-washing, try a superwash.

Superwash wool is chemically treated to remove or coat the scales and prevent felting and shrinking. It is also less itchy. Many of the sock yarns available have some elastic or nylon in them to improve the durability. If you put the effort into socks, you want them to last.

Acrylic yarn has come a long way in the last 10–20 years. However, it still is not the best fiber to use for socks to wear inside shoes or to do much walking.

Microfiber is another form of acrylic and does not wear well for socks. These fibers are inexpensive, easily washable and come in a great variety of colors and textures, but are best used for slippers or bed socks that do not have to withstand everyday use.

SELF-STRIPING YARN

Self-striping sock yarn is designed for knitting in stockinette stitch. Because crochet uses 30 percent more yarn, the stripes will come out differently than in knit socks. Knitting uses 1 basic stitch made in 2 directions. There are varieties of crochet stitches worked in countless combinations. These different stitches also use varying amounts of yarn and therefore affect the striping pattern. A slight variation in tension or stitch count will also affect the stripes. So, don't worry about getting the stripes or the color sequence the same on both socks. It is nice when they do match, but don't drive yourself crazy.

DECREASING

Many decreases are made by working single crochet decrease or by skipping a stitch. This leaves a hole.

BLIND DECREASE

Insert the hook into the front loop of each of the next 2 stitches and pull up a loop through both stitches at once. Then, finish the single crochet. Bravo—less of a hole.

FOUNDATION SINGLE CROCHET

Ch 2, insert hook in 2nd ch from hook, pull lp through, yo, pull through 1 lp on hook (*ch-1 completed*), yo, pull through all lps on hook (*sc completed*).

Here is the tricky part. Insert the hook into the ch-1 stitch between the lps and under the back bar. Pull up a lp and make a ch. Yo, then finish the sc.

To make the heel opening, sk the ch-2 at the beginning. Insert your hook in the same st as the last st made, pull up a lp and make the ch, then finish the sc. ■

rose quartz

DESIGN BY **KIM KOTARY**

SKILL LEVEL

INTERMEDIATE

FINISHED SIZES
Women's sock size given for 7–9 *(small)*; changes for 9–11 *(medium)* and 10–12 *(large)* are in [ ].

MATERIALS
- Super fine (sock) weight yarn (1¾ oz/230 yds/50g per ball): 2 [2, 3] balls purple variegated
- Size 4/2.00mm steel crochet hook or size needed to obtain gauge
- Tapestry needle
- Stitch markers

1 SUPER FINE

GAUGE
27 sc = 4 inches; 34 sc rows = 4 inches

PATTERN NOTES
Work in continuous rounds, do not turn or join unless otherwise stated.

Mark first stitch of each round.

Join with slip stitch as indicated unless otherwise stated.

INSTRUCTIONS

SOCK
MAKE 2.
TOE
Rnd 1: Ch 15, sc in 2nd ch from hook and in each ch across to last ch, 3 sc in last ch, place marker in center sc of sc group, working on opposite side of ch, sc in each ch across with 2 sc in last ch, place marker in last st, do not join *(see Pattern Notes)*. (30 sc)

Rnd 2: [2 sc in next st, sc in each st across to 1 st before next marker, 2 sc in next st, sc in marked st, move marker] around.

Next rnds: Rep rnd 2 until there are 46 [54, 62] sc.

Next rnds: Work even until piece measures 2 inches from beg. At end of last rnd, join *(see Pattern Notes)* in beg sc.

INSTEP
Rnd 1: *Sk next st, 3 dc in next st**, sk next st, sc in next st, rep from * around, ending last rep at **. *(12 [14, 16] dc groups)*

Rnd 2: Sc in center dc of each dc group and 3 dc in each sc around.

Next rnds: Rep rnd 2 until piece measures 7 [8½, 10] inches from beg. At end of last rnd, join in beg sc. Fasten off.

HEEL OPENING

Fold Toe flat, join in sc at fold, ch 26 [29, 33] sk next 24 [27, 31] sts, sl st next sc.

ANKLE

Rnd 1: Working in sts and chs, rep rnd 2 of Instep.

Next rnds: Rep rnd 2 of Instep until piece measures 14 [14, 15] inches from beg. At end of last rnd, join in beg sc.

CUFF

With WS facing, *ch 2, 5 dc in center dc of next dc group, ch 2**, sc in next sc, rep from * around, ending last rep at **, join in joining sl st of last rnd. Fasten off.

HEEL

Rnd 1: Join at 1 end of Heel Opening, place marker, evenly sp 50 [56, 64] sc around opening, place marker at each side of opening so there are 24 [27, 31] sts between markers.

Rnd 2: [Sc in each sc around to 2 sts before next marker, sc dec (*see Stitch Guide*) in next 2 sts, sc in marked st, move marker, sc dec in next 2 sts] around.

Next rnds: Rep rnd 2 until there are 30 sts. At end of last rnd, leaving long end, fasten off.

Turn Sock inside out and with long end, sew opening closed.

Turn right side out. ∎

Crochet symbols are a universal language that allows an alternative way of reading patterns.

THE SYMBOLS

In symbol crochet, each stitch is represented by a little picture or symbol.

⬯ or ◗ represents one chain (ch)—and looks pretty much like one.

+ represents one single crochet (sc).

T represents half double crochet (hdc).

Ŧ represents one double crochet (dc).

Ŧ represents one triple crochet (tr).

● represents one slip stitch (sl st)—the symbol is just like that for the chain, but is filled in.

 represents a 4-triple crochet cluster (4-tr cl).

These are the basic symbols we will use in the Melody Mini Doily practice project on the facing page.

Sometimes there is a special symbol for a group of stitches, such as a bobble or a popcorn; these symbols are given either with the pattern or are included in a stitch glossary.

A glossary of all symbols used in this book begins on page 84.

THE DIAGRAM

When symbols are arranged to form a "picture" of the work to be done, it is called a diagram. The diagram looks quite similar to the finished crocheted piece and shows at a glance just how it is constructed.

On circular designs such as doilies, the diagram is followed starting at the center, working from right to left (counterclockwise) if you are right-handed and from left to right (clockwise) if you are left-handed.

The number 6 in the center of the ring shows the number of chains needed to start; the symbol for slip stitch indicates joining in a ring. The number of the round is indicated at beginning of the round.

This mini doily practice piece will let you practice following the symbols and show how a diagram is made.

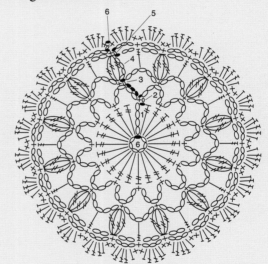

Melody Mini Doily

MELODY MINI DOILY

MATERIALS

Size 10 crochet cotton
Size 7/1.65mm steel crochet hook or size
   needed to obtain gauge

GAUGE

9 tr = 1 inch

PATTERN NOTES

In the table below, in the left column, you will find the symbols that tell you what to work for each row. In the right column of the table, the symbols are written out in words. First try to work from the symbols, then check your work against the words.

SYMBOL	WORDS
	Ch 6, sl st in first ch to form ring.
Rnd 1:	**Rnd 1:** Ch 4 *(counts as first tr)*, 23 tr in ring, join with sl st in 4th ch of beg ch-4. *(24 tr)*
Rnd 2:	**Rnd 2:** Ch 1, sc in same ch as joining, ch 5, *sk next tr, sc in next tr, ch 5, rep from * 10 times, join with sl st in beg sc. *(12 ch-5 sps)*
Rnd 3:	**Rnd 3:** Sl st in each of next 3 chs, ch 1, sc in same ch as last sl st, ch 5, [sc in 3rd ch of next ch-5 sp, ch 5] 11 times, join with sl st in beg sc.

Rnd 4:

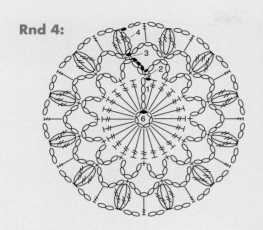

Rnd 4: Ch 4, keeping last lp of each tr on hook, 3 tr in same sc, yo and pull through all 4 lps on hook (*beg cl*), ch 2, tr in 3rd ch of next ch-5 sp, ch 2, keeping last lp of each tr on hook, 4 tr in next sc, yo and pull through all lps on hook (*cl*), ch 2, *tr in 3rd ch of next ch-5 sp, ch 2, cl in next sc, ch 2, rep from * 9 times, tr in 3rd ch of next ch-5 sp, ch 2, join with sl st in top of beg cl.

Rnd 5:

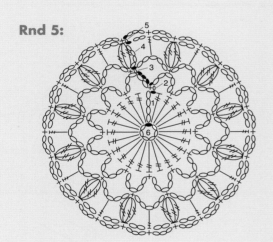

Rnd 5: Ch 1, sc in top of same beg cl, *ch 3, sc in next tr, ch 3, sc in top of next cl, rep from * 10 times, ch 3, sc in next tr, ch 3, join with sl st in beg sc. (*24 ch-3 sps*)

Rnd 6:

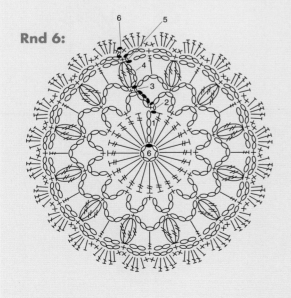

Rnd 6: Sl st in next ch-3 sp, ch 1, (sc, hdc, 3 dc, hdc, sc) in same ch sp and in each ch-3 sp around, join with sl st in beg sc. Fasten off. Secure ends. ■

SYMBOL GLOSSARY

SYMBOL	NAME		STITCH
⬯	U.S.	chain (ch)	
	U.K.	chain	
	Français	maille en l'air	
	Español	cadeneta (cad)	
	Deutsch	Luftmasche (Lftn)	
	Italiano	punto catenella	
+	U.S.	single crochet (sc)	
	U.K.	double crochet (dc)	
	Français	maille serrée	
	Español	punto bajo (pb)	
	Deutsch	Feste Masche (fM)	
	Italiano	maglia bassa (m. bassa)	
⊤	U.S.	double crochet (dc)	
	U.K.	treble (tr)	
	Français	bride (br)	
	Español	punto alto doble (pad)	
	Deutsch	Stäbchen (Stb)	
	Italiano	maglia alta (m. alta)	
⊤	U.S.	half double crochet (hdc)	
	U.K.	half treble (htr)	
	Français	demi-bride (demi-br)	
	Español	punto alto (pa)	
	Deutsch	Halbe Stäbchen (h.Stb)	
	Italiano	mexxa maglia alta	

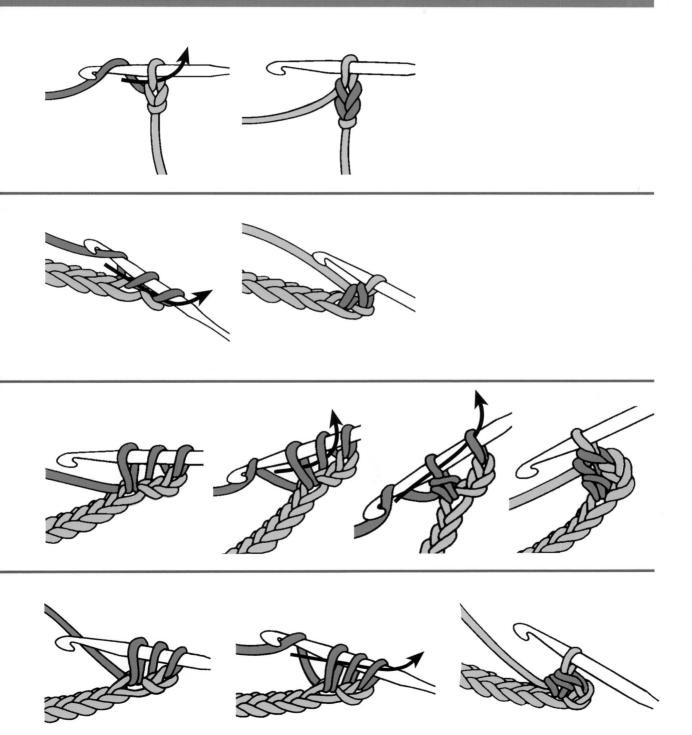

SYMBOL	NAME		STITCH
	U.S.	triple crochet (tr)	
	U.K.	double treble (dtr)	
	Français	doulble bride (d-br)	
	Español	punto alto triple (pat)	
	Deutsch	Doppel-Stäbchen (D.Stb)	
	Italiano	maglia ltissima	
	U.S.	slip stitch (sl st)	
	U.K.	slip stitch (sl st)	
	Français	maille coulee	
	Español	punto enano (pe)	
	Deutsch	Kettmasche	
	Italiano	maglia bassissima	
	U.S.	picot	
	U.K.	picot	
	Français	picot (pi)	
	Español	piquito	
	Deutsch	Pilot (Pi)	
	Italiano	Pippiolino	
	U.S.	cluster (cl)	
	U.K.	cluster (CL)	
	Français	grappe	
	Español	puntos altos cerrados en el mismo punto	
	Deutsch	Büschelmasche	
	Italiano	maglia raggruppata	

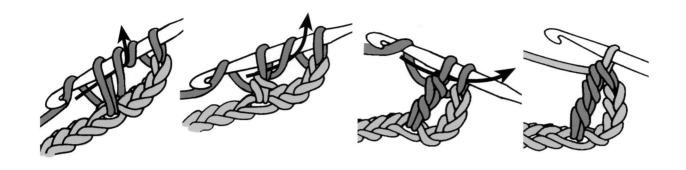

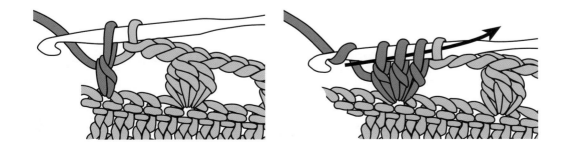

tunisian

Tunisian crochet requires a special Tunisian crochet hook, and the stitches are always held on the hook.

What is Tunisian crochet, and how is it different than regular crochet? Standard Tunisian crochet stitches are worked in an assembly-line fashion—i.e., the stitch loops are held on the hook and then worked off. For the first part of the row, you pick up and hold loops on the hook as you work across the row; for the second part, you work those loops off the hook. The various Tunisian stitches are created by way of the yarn over, where the hook is inserted, and how the loops are worked off the hook.

To accomplish Tunisian crochet, you will need a different kind of hook. A Tunisian crochet hook is longer than a regular crochet hook. It has a hook at 1 end and a knob at the other end to hold the stitches on the hook. Because Tunisian crochet hooks are available in various lengths (both straight and flexible), when trying to determine what length hook you need, select a hook that can hold a project that is up to 3 times longer than the hook. A flexible hook can be used for wider or heavier projects. This type of hook has a crochet hook on one end and a flexible cable between the hook and the knob on the other end. The cable allows a large number of stitches to be held on the length of the hook.

STITCHES
BASIC FOUNDATION ROW
1. **Work loops on hook:** (work lps on hook) Ch as stated, sk first ch (*see Photo 1A*),

2nd ch from hook

1A

insert hook in 2nd ch from hook (*see Photo 1B*),

1B

yo, pull lp through ch, holding all lps on hook *(you will now have 2 lps on hook—see Photo 1C),*

[insert hook in next ch, yo, pull lp through ch] across *(see Photo 1D).*

You will have the same number of lps on hook as number of chs in the Basic Foundation Row.

2. Work loops off hook: Ch 1 *(see Photo 2A),*

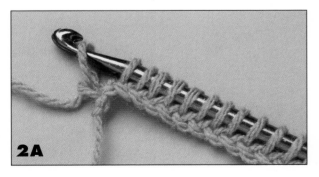

[yo, pull through 2 lps on hook *(see Photo 2B)*] across.

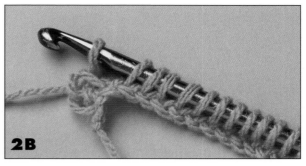

Last lp on hook is first lp of next row.

NOTE: *Typically to begin working lps off the hook in Tunisian most books will tell you to yo, pull through 1 lp, (yo and pull through 2 lps on hook) until all lps have been worked off the hook. However some patterns describe the first yo and pull through 1 lp, as a ch-1.*

TUNISIAN SIMPLE STITCH (TSS)

Ch as stated, work Basic Foundation Row *(see Photos 1A–2B).*

Sk first vertical bar, insert hook under front vertical bar from right to left *(see Photo 3A),*

yo, pull up lp (see Photo 3B),

[insert hook under next vertical bar from right to left, yo, pull up lp] across.

At end of row, work into ch-1 from previous row, insert hook under both front and back lps (see Stitch Guide) of ch-1 (see Photo 3C),

yo and pull up lp. You should now have same number of lps on hook as starting ch.

Work lps off hook (see Photos 2A–2B). Last lp on hook is first lp of next row.

TUNISIAN KNIT STITCH (TKS)

Ch as stated, work Basic Foundation Row (see Photos 1A–2B).

Sk first vertical bar, insert hook from front to back (see Photo 4A),

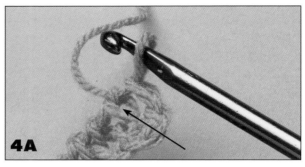

between front and back vertical bars (see Photo 4B) of same st,

yo, pull lp through (see Photo 4C), hold all lps on hook as you work across the row.

At end of row, work into ch-1 from previous row, insert hook under both front and back lps of ch-1 (see Photo 3C), yo and pull up lp. You should now have same number of lps on hook as starting ch.

Work lps off hook (see Photos 2A–2B). Last lp on hook is first lp of next row.

TUNISIAN DOUBLE STITCH (TDS)

TDS completed stitch

Note: *Insertion of hook shown here is as for knit stitch. This stitch can also be created using other insertion points if desired.*

Ch as stated, work Basic Foundation Row *(see Photos 1A–2B).*

Ch 2 at beginning of row, sk first vertical bar, yo, insert hook from front to back *(see Photo 5A),*

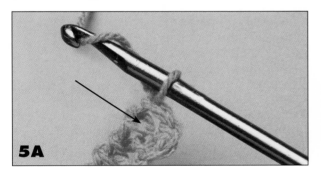

5A

between front and back vertical bars *(see Photo 5B)* of same st,

5B

yo, pull lp through *(see Photo 5C),*

5C

yo, pull through 2 lps on hook *(see Photo 5D),* holding all lps on hook across your work. ■

5D

necklace & earrings

DESIGN BY **ANNETTE STEWART**

SKILL LEVEL

EASY

FINISHED SIZES

Necklace: 21 inches

Earrings: 2 inches

MATERIALS

- Omega La Espiga #18 nylon (7 oz/197 yds/200g per ball):
  1 ball #67 variegated green
- Size H/8/5mm afghan hook or size needed to obtain gauge
- Size H/8/5mm crochet hook
- Tapestry needle
- 1-inch surgical steel fishhook earrings: 1 pair

GAUGE

Afghan hook: 7 sts = 1¼ inches; 3 rows = 1¼ inches

SPECIAL STITCHES

Work loops off hook (work lps off hook): Yo, pull through 1 lp on hook (*see A on Illustration*), [yo, pull through 2 lps on hook] across, leaving 1 lp on hook at end of row (*see B on Illustration*).

A

B

Afghan Stitch

Knit stitch (knit st): With yarn in back, insert hook from front to back (*see Illustration*).

Afghan Knit Stitch

INSTRUCTIONS

NECKLACE

Row 1: Leaving 10-inch end, with afghan hook, ch 75, insert hook in 2nd ch from hook, yo, pull lp through, leaving all lps on hook, [insert hook in next ch, yo, pull lp through] across, work lps off hook (*see Special Stitches*).

Row 2: Sk first vertical bar, knit st *(see Special Stitches)* across, work lps off hook.

Rows 3–5: Rep row 2.

BUTTON
Ch 5, 10 sc in 2nd ch from hook. Leaving 50-inch end, fasten off.

FINISHING
Weave end through top of sc, pull to close, insert needle from top to bottom through center of Button and rem chs. Secure end on back of Button, do not fasten off.

Allow rows of Necklace to roll closed. The rows lie at an angle; Leave angle in place as you sew the 2 edges tog to close, sewing first st on bottom to the 3rd st on top. This will cause a slight spiral.

Sew end closed and continue sewing.

With 10-inch end, make lp about 1 inch long at the 2nd end of Necklace. Sew 1 st in end to secure, and then wrap several times through lp. Fasten off and secure end.

EARRING
MAKE 2.
Row 1: Leaving 8-inch end, with afghan hook, ch 7, pull up lp in 2nd ch from hook and in each ch across, work lps off hook *(see Special Stitches)*.

Rows 2 & 3: Sk first vertical bar, **knit st** *(see Special Stitches)* across, work off lps. Leaving 12-inch end, fasten off.

FINISHING
Thread end through eye of fishhook earring. Secure end by working 2 sts to fix in place.

The rows lie at slight angle; leave angle in place as you close the end and sew 2 edges tog to close.

The first st on bottom will be sewn to 2nd st on top; this will cause a slight spiral.

Sew opposite end closed. Fasten off. ■

waffle-weave

Waffle-weave is a stitch that forms a thick, stretchy, interlocking double layer of fabric. The interlocking of two layers produces a dimpled surface that looks like a waffle-iron imprint.

The dimples trap air into little pockets which creates a fabric that is very warm. It is the air pockets, not the tightness, thickness or weight of the yarn/crochet, that contribute to the warmth.

The right side of the fabric shows on both front and back. This makes pieces reversible.

GAUGE

Obtaining an accurate gauge is difficult in this stitch because the stitch is so stretchy and the interlocking causes the fabric to shrink in over the first few rows. Make a large swatch and measure the gauge near the top. If you are part way through a project and find your gauge is off slightly, even though you made a swatch and are working to the swatch specifications, you will probably be OK because the fabric is so stretchy.

PATTERN NOTES

You work through the front loops when making the waffle-weave stitch. Front and back loops are named from the side of the crochet facing you—when you turn your work, what was a front loop becomes a back loop and vice versa!

The front of the fabric is the side facing you at the moment. The back of the fabric is the side away from you at the moment. These change when you turn your work!

The right side of the fabric is the side that is the good side or outside when a project is completed. The wrong side of the fabric is the bad side, back side or inside.

THE STITCH

The waffle-weave stitch is worked back and forth (i.e., with turns) even when working in the round as for a hat. Use a knife (palm) grip to reduce hand fatigue. Switch to the knife grip even if you use a pencil grip for your other crochet.

You will be using hooks that may seem too large for the yarn weight. However, smaller hooks cause the fabric to be stiff and reduce the size of the air pockets so the fabric is not as warm.

To learn the waffle-weave stitch, make a beg ch of 14 chs.

Row 1: Sk first ch, sc in front lp *(see Photo A)* of each ch across, turn.

A   Front lps of beg ch

Row 2: Ch 1, *insert hook from bottom to top under front lp of beg ch (see Photo B) *(this was the back bar of beg ch that was not used in row 1, it became the front lp when you turned your work)*, insert hook from bottom to top under front lp of sc of row 1 directly above ch, yo, pull through 2 front lps, yo and pull through 2 lps on hook, rep from * across, turn.

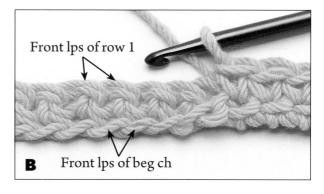

Front lps of row 1

B   Front lps of beg ch

In the project instructions, this is written [sc dec *(see Stitch Guide)* front lp of beg ch and row 1] across, turn.

Row 3: Ch 1, *insert hook from bottom to top under front lp of sc in row 1 (see Photo C) *(2 rows previous, the front lps form a horizontal line across the bottom of the piece)*, insert hook from bottom to top under front lp of sc in row 2 *(previous row)*, yo, pull through 2 front lps, yo and pull through 2 lps on hook, rep from * across, turn.

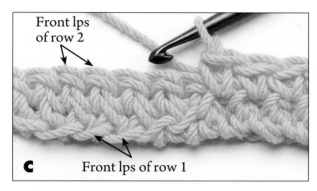

Front lps of row 2

C Front lps of row 1

In project instructions, this is written [sc dec in front lp from 2 rows previous and front lp from previous row] across, turn.

Row 4: Ch 1, *insert hook from bottom to top under front lp of sc 2 rows previous (see Photo D) *(front lps form a horizontal row)*, insert hook from bottom to top under front lp of sc in previous row, yo, pull through 2 front lps, yo and pull through 2 lps on hook, rep from * across, turn.

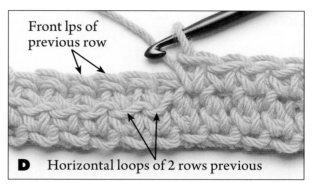

Front lps of previous row

D Horizontal loops of 2 rows previous

Rep row 4 for desired length.

In project instructions, this is written [sc dec in front lp from 2 rows previous and front lp from previous row] across or work in waffle-weave pattern.

Last row bind-off): Ch 1, [sc to front lp from 2 rows previous and both front and back lps from previous row] across. Fasten off. ∎

waffle-weave
soft rainbow scarf

DESIGN BY **NANCY NEHRING**

SKILL LEVEL

EASY

FINISHED SIZE
4 x 80 inches

MATERIALS
- Light (light worsted) weight yarn: 5 oz/372 yds/150g variegated 1½ oz/111 yds/45g lime green
- Size K/10½/6.5mm crochet hook or size needed to obtain gauge
- 3 x 4-inch piece of cardboard
- Tapestry needle

3 LIGHT

GAUGE
12 waffle-weave sts = 4 inches

INSTRUCTIONS

SCARF

Row 1: With variegated and leaving 12-inch end, ch 13, sk first ch, sc in front lp *(see Stitch Guide)* of each rem ch, turn. *(12 sc)*

Row 2: Ch 1, [sc dec *(see Stitch Guide)* in front lp of beg ch and row 1] across, turn.

Row 3: Ch 1, [sc dec in front lp from 2 rows previous and front lp from previous row] across, turn.

Next rows: Rep row 3 until about 3 feet of yarn remains.

Last row: Ch 1, [sc dec in front lp from 2 rows previous and both front and back lps *(see Stitch Guide)* from previous row] across. Fasten off.

POMPOM
MAKE 2.

Cut a piece of cardboard 3 x 4 inches. Cut a U into 1 short side leaving ½-inch sides.

Cut a 24-inch length of lime green yarn and place over base of U. Referring to Illustration, wrap lime green yarn around cardboard 200 times, piling it upon itself. Tie yarn strand at base of U tightly around center of wraps. Cut wraps apart along edges of cardboard. Trim Pompom to shape.

FINISHING

With tapestry needle, weave beg yarn end in and out of bottom lps of beg ch. Pull tight to gather and knot to secure. Rep on opposite end, weaving yarn end in and out of top lps of last row. Sew 1 Pompom to each end of scarf. ∎

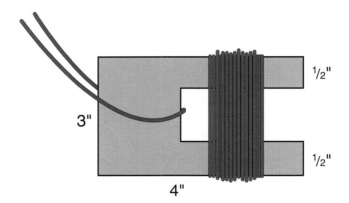

wiggly crochet

Wiggly crochet is a 3-dimensional crochet that was popular in the 1950s for hot pads. The thickness of the final product made it a good insulator. In the projects presented here, we will also use the thick property of this crochet as cushioning and as pure decoration.

Wiggly crochet begins with a base mesh made up of chain stitches in the horizontal direction and double crochet stitches in the vertical direction. This is the same mesh used in filet crochet. Then the 3-D aspect is added by working 3–5 double crochets over each bar of the mesh base. These double crochets are packed so closely together that they have no choice but to stand out away from the mesh.

The double crochets that traditionally make up the "wiggle" are worked in concentric circles with the last double crochet of the circle joined to the first. But you can let the circles wander more to create more complex geometric and realistic patterns.

Any size or weight of yarn can be used for wiggly crochet.

Pure cotton yarn is good for hot pads and casserole mats. Other types of yarn may melt or burn if exposed to high temperatures. For bath mats, cotton is also an ideal choice, with it being the most absorbent of fibers.

Hot pads and casserole mats require smooth, hard yarns to provide an even, durable surface with a sure grip. Cotton yarns with more interesting properties than the usual size 10 crochet cotton can be used effectively for wiggly crochet.

MESH BASE

Most projects use a square or rectangular mesh base (see Photo A). However, some projects use shaped or tubular mesh bases.

The mesh base is crocheted in rows of squares. Each square is formed over the square below, using a combination of a double crochet stitch and a chain-2.

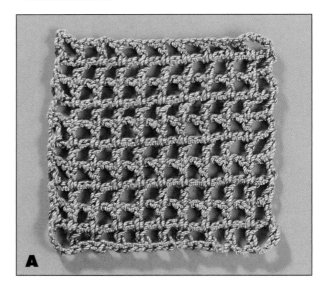

A

Make this practice mesh base of 10 x 10 squares as follows:

Row 1: Ch 35, dc in 8th ch from hook (first 7 chs count as a ch-2 sp, dc and ch-2 sp), *ch 2, sk next 2 chs, dc in next ch, rep from * across, turn.

Row 2: Ch 5 (counts as first dc and ch-2 sp on this and following rows), *ch 2, sk next ch-2 sp, dc in next dc, rep from * to ch-7 chs, ch 2, sk next 2 chs, dc in next ch, turn.

Row 3: Ch 5, *sk next ch-2 sp, dc in next dc, rep from * to turning ch-5, ch 2, sk next 2 chs of turning ch-5, dc in next ch, turn.

Rows 4–10: Rep row 3. At end of last row, fasten off.

Measure the mesh base in each direction. When most people work a base mesh with their normal tension, the spaces in the mesh do not come out square. The spaces in the mesh need to be as square as possible. Practice making the spaces square by adjusting your tension. An example is to work the 2 chains tightly and the double crochet loosely to make squares or doing just the opposite. Practice adjusting your tension until your mesh is as square as possible. It will be hard at first but will become second nature with a little practice.

WIGGLES

The "wiggles" are formed by 3–5 double crochet stitches worked over each bar formed by a chain-2 or double crochet on the mesh base (see Photo B). More double crochet stitches used on each bar make it thicker and more wiggly. 3 double crochet stitches form a top that is so thin, you can see light through it, and it forms rather straight lines that follow the grid of the mesh base. But the finished project is lighter in weight because it uses less yarn than one with 5 double crochet stitches over each bar.

On the other hand, 5 double crochet stitches form a thick top where the double crochet stitches on each bar overfill the bar and have to curve back and forth to fit in their space. 5 double crochet stitches also stretch the bars to their maximum length, thus helping form square shapes even if the squares of the mesh base are slightly rectangular. Also, when working thicker yarns over a base mesh of thinner yarn, fewer double crochet stitches are needed on each bar.

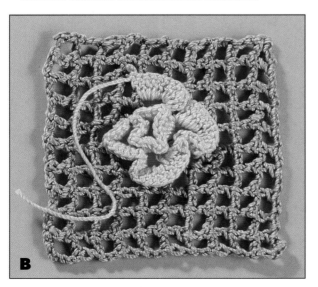

B

To access a bar, fold the bars above and below it down so that the bar being worked on pops up. The working yarn always stays on top of the mesh base. Join the yarn around a bar and chain 2. This counts as the first double crochet. Work remaining double crochet stitches over the same bar.

The direction of flow from one bar to the next as well as the color of yarn is shown on a chart accompanying each project. In most cases, the wiggles are worked in continuous loops that wander about. These are called "circles" in the instructions, although they are far from round in some cases. Unless otherwise noted in a pattern, begin anywhere on the circle and work either clockwise or counterclockwise as desired. The last double crochet stitch of the circle is usually joined to the beginning with a slip stitch in the 2nd chain made at the beginning of the circle. However, some circles may not be joined.

The large colored rectangles on the chart indicate the color of yarn to use. The little lines between large rectangles indicate direction of flow, what direction to go to get from one bar to the next. You must follow these precisely or you may not be able to fill in all of the bars for the entire project. If you have trouble following the chart on the front of your work, turn your work over. It is easier to see which bars are covered and which are not on the back of the work.

Generally, every bar of the base mesh will have wiggles covering it. This is important for items like hot pads, or you may burn your fingers where there is an open bar.

There are 2 exceptions to covering all bars. The first is the outer edge of the base mesh. Here only every other bar will be covered. These open outer bars can be covered with an edge finish if you want a "complete" look. The second is in purely decorative patterns where part of the mesh base is left uncovered by choice.

GAUGE

Work a swatch with both base mesh and wiggles to determine your gauge. When you complete your base mesh, it will probably be significantly smaller than the final size of the project given in the instructions. The mesh is very stretchy and impossible to measure for gauge. The size of the swatch or final project is sometimes controlled by your tension while forming the base mesh but generally by the number of double crochet stitches worked over each bar. 5 double crochet stitches stretch each bar to its full extent. 3 double crochet stitches leave the bar loose so that your tension while forming the base mesh may come into play.

Gauge is difficult to control in wiggly crochet. If you are much looser or much tighter than the gauge listed in the instructions, you may not have enough yarn, you may have too much yarn for the project or your project may be too loose or too stiff. In this case, try changing

hook sizes for the base mesh, try working more or fewer double crochets over each bar, or try a combination of the two.

EDGING

When all of the wiggles are filled in on the mesh base, every other bar around the outside edge is "open" or unused with no double crochet stitches covering it.

For a finished look, most projects require an edging to be worked over these bars. Instructions are given when an edging is needed. ∎

wiggly crochet
quilt rug

DESIGN BY **SUSAN LOWMAN**

SKILL LEVEL

INTERMEDIATE

FINISHED SIZE
27½ x 42 inches

MATERIALS
- Red Heart Luster Sheen fine (sport) weight yarn (4 oz/335 yds/113g per skein):
  2 skeins #2 black
- Red Heart Super Saver medium (worsted) weight yarn (7 oz/364 yds/198g per skein):
  2 skeins #360 café
  1 skein each #365 coffee, #376 burgundy, #256 carrot, #321 gold, #406 medium thyme and #356 amethyst
- Size E/4/3.5mm and H/8/5mm crochet hooks or size needed to obtain gauge

2
FINE

4
MEDIUM

GAUGE
Size E hook and fine weight yarn: 4 mesh = 2 inches; 5 mesh rows = 2 inches

PATTERN NOTES
Use fine weight yarn and size E hook for Foundation Mesh, and medium weight yarn and size H hook for wiggly crochet.

Use rug backing on back of rugs that are placed on floors other than carpet.

Join with slip stitch as indicated unless otherwise stated.

Chain-5 at beginning of row or round counts as first double crochet and chain-2 unless otherwise stated.

Chain-3 at beginning of row or round counts as first double crochet unless otherwise stated.

SPECIAL STITCH
Mesh: Ch 2, sk next 2 chs, dc in next ch or st.

INSTRUCTIONS

RUG
FOUNDATION MESH
Row 1 (RS): With size E hook and black, ch 212, dc in 8th ch from hook *(first mesh)*, mesh *(see Special Stitch)* across, turn. *(69 mesh)*

Rows 2–49: Ch 5 *(see Pattern Notes)*, sk next 2 chs, dc in next st, mesh across, turn. At end of last row, fasten off.

Mesh will measure approximately 20 x 34 inches and will stretch when wiggly crochet is worked.

WIGGLY CROCHET
1. With RS facing and size H hook, join *(see Pattern Notes)* coffee in last mesh on row 49 at dot on Chart *(see Chart on page 102)* in top left corner, ch 3 *(see Pattern Notes)*, dc in same mesh, working 2 dc around each dc post and in each ch-2 sp, follow path on chart around to beg with 4 dc in each corner ch-5 sp, join in 3rd ch of beg ch-3. Fasten off.

With size H hook, work additional border rounds in same manner, beg at each dot in top left corner on chart and following path around to beg, join in 3rd ch of beg ch-3. Fasten off.

Work other sections in same manner, beg at each dot on chart and following path around to beg, join in 3rd ch of beg ch-3. Fasten off. ∎

COLOR KEY
Coffee
Café
Burgundy
Carrot
Gold
Medium thyme
Amethyst

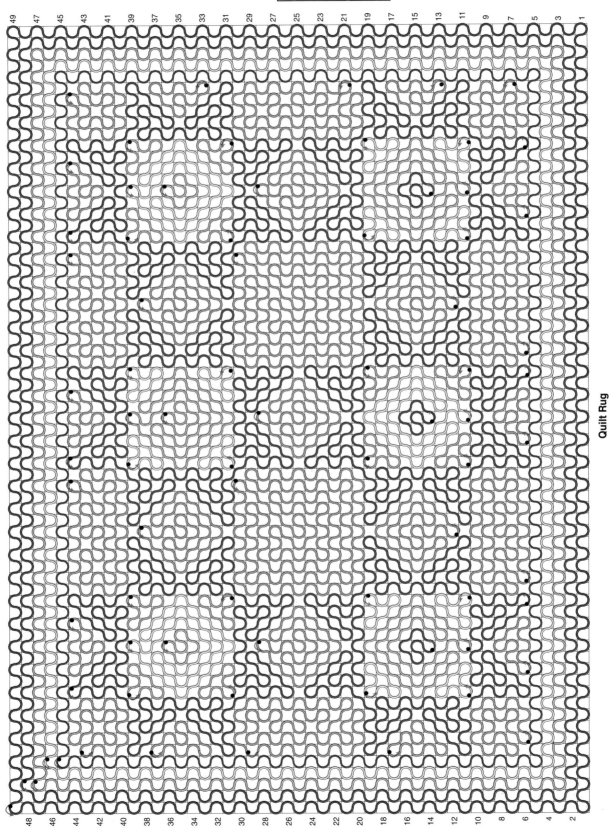

Quilt Rug
Chart

crochet basics

Whether you are just learning or need a refresher course, you can learn all the basic techniques of crochet by following our easy lesson plan. Each step is illustrated with large, step-by-step diagrams. It's as if we're sitting there beside you giving you hints and special helps along the way.

LESSON 1: GETTING STARTED

To crochet, you need only a crochet hook, some yarn and a tapestry needle.

YARN

Yarn comes in many sizes, from fine crochet cotton used for doilies, to wonderful bulky mohairs used for afghans and sweaters. The most commonly used yarn is medium (or worsted) weight. It is readily available in a wide variety of beautiful colors. This is the weight we will use in our lessons. Always read yarn labels carefully. The label will tell you how many ounces, grams, meters and/or yards of yarn are in the skein or ball of yarn. Read the label to find out the fiber content of the yarn, its washability, and sometimes, how to pull the yarn from the skein. Also, there is usually a dye-lot number on the label. This number assures you that the color of each skein with this number is the same. Yarn of the same color name may vary in shade somewhat from dye lot to dye lot, creating variations in color when a project is completed.

Therefore, when purchasing yarn for a project, it is important to match the dye-lot numbers on the skeins.

You'll need a blunt-point sewing needle with an eye big enough to carry the yarn for weaving in yarn ends and sewing seams. This is a size 16 steel tapestry needle. You can buy big plastic needles called yarn needles, but they are not as good as the steel needles.

HOOKS

Crochet hooks come in many sizes, from very fine steel hooks, used to make intricate doilies and lace, to very large ones of plastic or wood, used to make bulky sweaters or rugs.

The hooks you will use most often are made of aluminum, are about 6 inches long and are sized alphabetically by letter from B (*smallest*) to K. For our lessons, you'll need a size H hook, which is considered a medium-size hook.

The aluminum crochet hook looks like this:

In Illustration 1, (A) is the hook end, which is used to hook the yarn and pull it through other loops of yarn (*called stitches*). (B) is the throat, a shaped area that helps you slide the stitch up onto (C) the working area.

(D) is the fingerhold, a flattened area that helps you grip the hook comfortably, usually with your thumb and middle finger; and (E) is the handle, which rests under your fourth and little fingers, and provides balance for easy, smooth work.

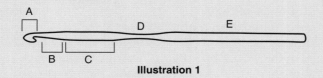

Illustration 1

It is important that every stitch is made on the working area, never on the throat (*which would make the stitch too tight*) and never on the fingerhold (*which would stretch the stitch*).

The hook is held in the right hand, with the thumb and third finger on the fingerhold, and the index finger near the tip of the hook (*see Illustration 2*).

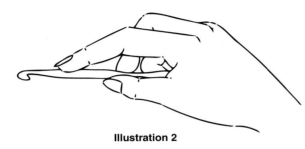

Illustration 2

The hook should be turned slightly toward you, not facing up or down. Illustration 3 shows how the hook is held, viewing from underneath the hand. The hook should be held firmly, but not tightly.

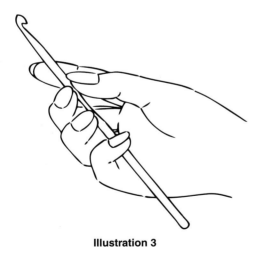

Illustration 3

LESSON 2: CHAIN STITCH (ABBREVIATED CH)

Crochet usually begins with a series of chain stitches called a beginning or foundation chain. Begin by making a slip knot on the hook about 6 inches from the free end of the yarn. Loop the yarn as shown in Illustration 4.

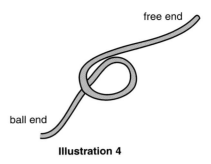

free end

ball end

Illustration 4

Insert the hook through center of loop and hook the free end (*see Illustration 5*).

Illustration 5

Pull this through and up onto the working area of the hook (*see Illustration 6*).

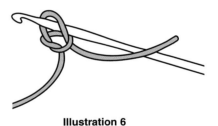

Illustration 6

Pull the free yarn end to tighten the loop (*see Illustration 7*).

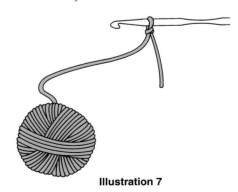

Illustration 7

The loop on the hook should be firm, but loose enough to slide back and forth easily on the hook. Be sure you still have about a 6-inch yarn end. Hold the hook, now with its slip knot, in your right hand (*see Illustration 8*).

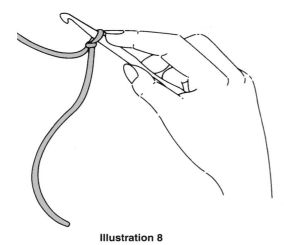

Illustration 8

Now let's make the first chain stitch.

Step 1: Hold the base of the slip knot with the thumb and index finger of your left hand, and thread yarn from the skein over the middle finger *(see Illustration 9)* and under the remaining fingers of the left hand *(see Illustration 9a)*.

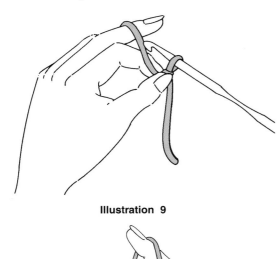

Illustration 9

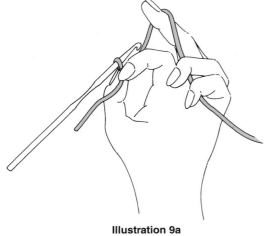

Illustration 9a

Your middle finger will stick up a bit to help the yarn feed smoothly from the skein/ball, and the other fingers help maintain an even tension on the yarn as you work.

Hint: As you practice, you can adjust the way your left hand holds the yarn to however is most comfortable for you.

Step 2: Bring the yarn over the hook from back to front and hook it *(see Illustration 10)*.

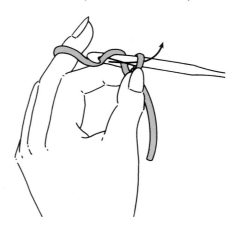

Illustration 10

Pull hooked yarn through the loop of the slip knot on the hook and up onto the working area of the hook *(see arrow on Illustration 10)*, you have now made 1 chain stitch *(see Illustration 11)*.

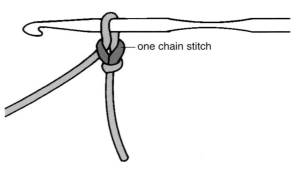

one chain stitch

Illustration 11

Step 3: *Again bring the yarn over the hook from back to front (see Illustration 12a).*

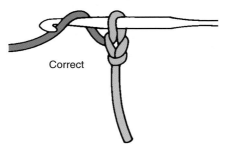

Illustration 12a

Correct

Note: *Take care not to bring yarn from front to back (see Illustration 12b).*

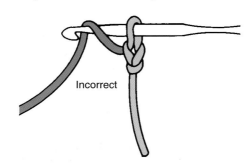

Incorrect

Illustration 12b

Hook it and pull through loop on the hook: You have made another chain stitch (*see Illustration 13*).

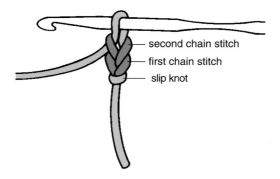

— second chain stitch
— first chain stitch
— slip knot

Illustration 13

Repeat step 3 for each additional chain stitch, being careful to move the left thumb and index finger up the chain close to the hook after each new stitch or two (*see Illustration 14a*). This helps you control the work. *Note: Illustration 14b shows the incorrect way to hold the stitches.* Also, be sure to pull each new stitch up onto the working area of the hook.

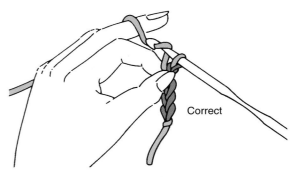

Correct

Illustration 14a

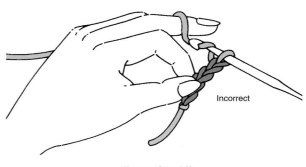

Incorrect

Illustration 14b

The working yarn and the work in progress are always held in your left hand.

Practice making chains until you are comfortable with your grip of the hook and the flow of the yarn. In the beginning your work will be uneven, with some chain stitches loose and others tight. While you're learning, try to keep the chain stitches loose. As your skill increases, the chain should be firm, but not tight, with all chain stitches even in size.

Hint: As you practice, if the hook slips out of a stitch, don't get upset! Just insert the hook again from the front into the center of the last stitch taking care not to twist the loop (*see Illustration 15*).

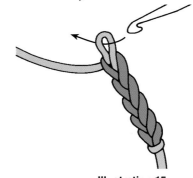

Illustration 15

When you are comfortable with the chain stitch, pull your hook out of the last stitch and pull out the work back to the beginning. Now you've learned the important first step of crochet—the beginning chain.

LESSON 3: WORKING INTO THE CHAIN

Once you have worked the beginning chain, you are ready to begin the stitches required to make any project. These stitches are worked into the foundation chain. For practice, make 6 chains loosely.

Hint: When counting your chain stitches at the start of a pattern—which you must do very carefully before continuing—note that the loop on the hook is never counted as a stitch, and the starting slip knot is never counted as a stitch *(see Illustration 16).*

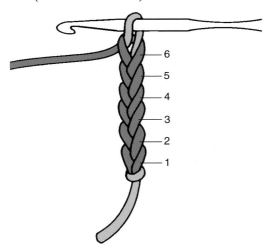

Illustration 16

Now stop and look at the chain. The front looks like a series of interlocking V's *(see Illustration 16),* and each stitch has a bump or ridge at the back *(see Illustration 17).*

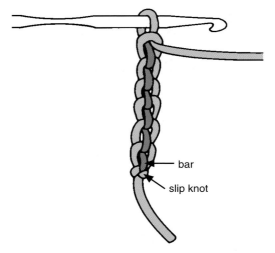

Illustration 17

You will never work into the first chain from the hook. Depending on the stitch, you will work into the second, third, fourth, etc., chain from the hook. The instructions will always state how many chains to skip before starting the first stitch.

When working a stitch, insert hook from the front of the chain, through the center of the "V" and under the corresponding bump on the back of the same stitch *(see Illustration 18).*

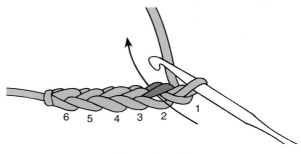

Illustration 18

Excluding the first stitch, you will work into every stitch in the chain unless the pattern states differently, but not into the starting slip knot *(see Illustration 18a).* Be sure that you do not skip that last chain at the end.

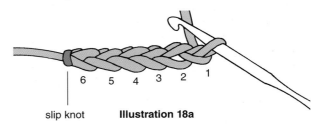

Illustration 18a

LESSON 4: SINGLE CROCHET (ABBREVIATED SC)

Most crochet is made with variations on just 4 different stitches: single crochet, double crochet, half double crochet and treble crochet. The stitches differ mainly in height, which is varied by the number of times the yarn is wrapped around the hook. The shortest and most basic of these stitches is the single crochet stitch.

WORKING ROW 1

To practice, begin with the chain of 6 stitches made in Lesson 3 and work the first row of single crochet as follows:

Step 1: Skip first chain stitch from hook. Insert hook in the 2nd chain stitch through the center of the "V" and under the back bump; with middle finger of left hand, bring yarn over the hook from back to front, and hook the yarn (*see Illustration 19*).

Illustration 19

Pull yarn through the chain stitch and well up onto the working area of the hook. You now have two loops on the hook (*see Illustration 20*).

Illustration 20

Step 2: Again bring yarn over the hook from back to front, hook it and pull it through both loops on the hook (*see Illustration 21*).

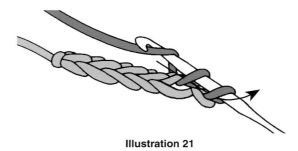

Illustration 21

One loop will remain on hook, and you have made one single crochet (*see Illustration 22*).

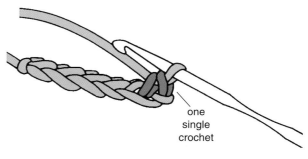

one single crochet

Illustration 22

Step 3: Insert hook in next chain stitch as before, hook the yarn and pull it through the chain stitch; hook the yarn again and pull it through both loops. You have made another single crochet.

Repeat step 3 in each remaining chain stitch, taking care to work in the last chain stitch, but not in the slip knot. You have completed one row of single crochet, and should have 5 stitches in the row. Illustration 23 shows how to count the stitches.

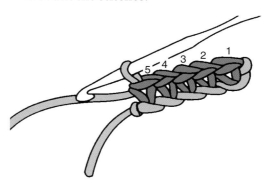

Illustration 23

Hint: As you work, be careful not to twist the chain; keep all the V's facing you.

WORKING ROW 2

To work the 2nd row of single crochet, you need to turn the work in the direction of the arrow (*counterclockwise*), as shown in Illustration 24, so you can work back across the first row.

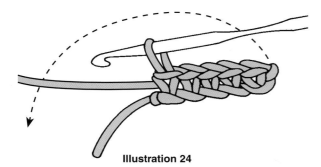

Illustration 24

Do not remove the hook from the loop as you do this (*see Illustration 24a*).

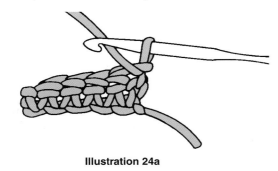

Illustration 24a

Now you need to bring the yarn up to the correct height to work the first stitch. So, to raise the yarn, chain 1 (*this is called a turning chain*).

This row, and all the following rows of single crochet, will be worked into a previous row of single crochet, not into the beginning chain as you did before. Remember that when you worked into the starting chain, you inserted the hook through the center of the "V" and under the bump. This is only done when working into a starting chain.

To work into a previous row of crochet, insert the hook under both loops of the previous stitch, as shown in Illustration 25, instead of through the center of the "V."

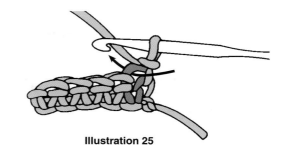

Illustration 25

The first single crochet of the row is worked in the last stitch of the previous row (*see Illustration 25*), not into the turning chain. Work a single crochet into each single crochet to the end, taking care to work in each stitch, especially the last stitch, which is easy to miss (*see Illustration 26*).

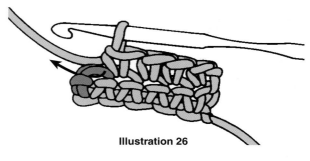

Illustration 26

Stop now and count your stitches; you should still have 5 single crochet on the row (*see Illustration 27*).

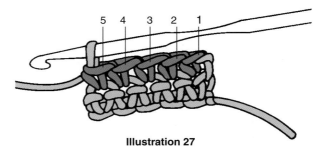

Illustration 27

Hint: When you want to pause to count stitches, check your work, have a snack or chat on the phone, you can remove your hook from the work—but do this at the end of a row, not in the middle.

To remove the hook, pull straight up on the hook to make a long loop (see Illustration 28). Then withdraw the hook and put it on a table or other safe place (sofas and chairs have a habit of eating crochet hooks).

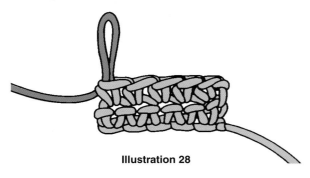

Illustration 28

Put work in a safe place so loop is not pulled out. To begin work again, just insert the hook in the big loop (don't twist the loop), and pull on the yarn from the skein to tighten the loop.

To end row 2, after the last single crochet, turn the work counterclockwise.

Here is the way instructions for row 2 might be written in a pattern:

Note: To save space, a number of abbreviations are used. For a list of abbreviations used in patterns, see page 134.

Row 2: Ch 1, sc in each sc across, turn.

WORKING ROW 3
Row 3 is worked exactly as you worked row 2. Here are the instructions as they would be given in a pattern:

Row 3: Rep row 2.

Now, wasn't that easy? For practice, work 3 more rows, which means you will repeat row 2 three times more.

Hint: Try to keep your stitches as smooth and even as possible. Remember to work loosely rather than tightly and to make each stitch well up on the working area of the hook. Be sure to turn at the end of each row and to check carefully to be sure you've worked into the last stitch of each row.

Count the stitches at the end of each row; do you still have 5? Good work.

Hint: What if you don't have 5 stitches at the end of a row? Perhaps you worked 2 stitches in 1 stitch, or skipped a stitch. Find your mistake, then just pull out your stitches back to the mistake, pulling out in crochet is simple.

Just take out the hook and gently pull on the yarn. The stitches will come out easily, when you reach the place where you want to start again, insert the hook in the last loop (taking care not to twist it) and begin.

FASTENING OFF
It's time to move on to another stitch, so let's fasten off your single crochet practice piece, which you can keep for future reference. After the last stitch of the last row, leaving a 6-inch end, cut the yarn. As you did when you took your hook out for a break, pull the hook straight up, but this time pull the yarn cut end completely through the stitch. Photo A shows an actual sample of 6 rows of single crochet to which you can compare your practice rows. It also shows how to count the stitches and rows.

Now you can put the piece away, and it won't pull out (you might want to tag this piece as a sample of single crochet).

LESSON 5: DOUBLE CROCHET (ABBREVIATED DC)

Double crochet is a taller stitch than single crochet. To practice, first chain 14 stitches loosely. Then work the first row of double crochet as follows:

WORKING ROW 1

Step 1: Bring yarn once over the hook from back to front (*as though you were going to make another chain stitch*), skip the first 3 chains from the hook, then insert hook in the 4th chain (*see Illustration 29*).

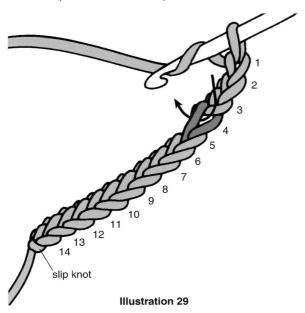

Illustration 29

Remember not to count the loop on the hook as a chain. Be sure to go through the center of the "V" of the chain and under the bump at the back, and do not twist the chain.

Step 2: Hook yarn and pull it through the chain stitch and up onto the working area of the hook; you now have three loops on hook (*see Illustration 30*).

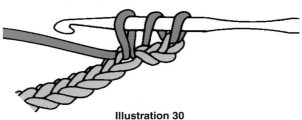

Illustration 30

Step 3: Hook yarn and pull through first 2 loops on the hook (*see Illustration 31*).

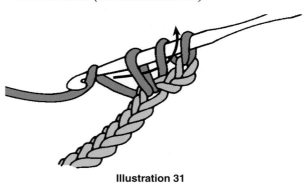

Illustration 31

You now have 2 loops on the hook (*see Illustration 32*).

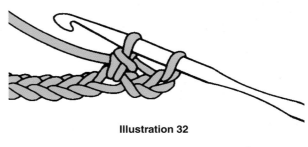

Illustration 32

Step 4: Hook yarn and pull through both loops on the hook (*see Illustration 33*).

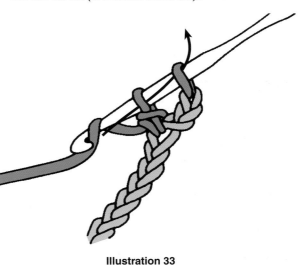

Illustration 33

You have now completed 1 double crochet and 1 loop remains on the hook (*see Illustration 34*).

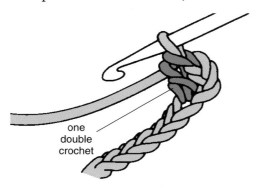

Illustration 34

Repeat steps 1–4 in each chain stitch across (*except in step 1, work in next chain, don't skip 3 chains*).

When you've worked a double crochet in the last chain, pull out your hook and look at your work. Then count your double crochet stitches. There should be 12 of them, counting the first 3 chain stitches you skipped at the beginning of the row as a double crochet (*see Illustration 35*).

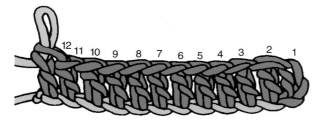

Illustration 35

Hint: In working double crochet on a beginning chain row, the 3 chains skipped before making the first double crochet is usually counted as a double crochet stitch.

Turn the work counterclockwise before beginning row 2.

WORKING ROW 2

To work row 2, you need to bring the thread up to the correct height for the next row. To raise the yarn, chain 3 (*this is called the turning chain*).

The 3 chains in the turning chain just made count as the first double crochet of the new row, so skip the first double crochet and work a double crochet in the 2nd stitch. Be sure to insert hook under top 2 loops of stitch. Illustrations 36a and 36b indicate the correct and incorrect placement of this stitch.

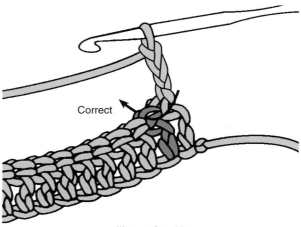

Illustration 36a

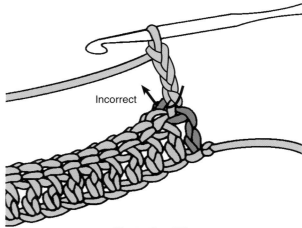

Illustration 36b

Work a double crochet in each remaining stitch across the previous row; at the end of each row, be sure to work the last double crochet in the top of the turning chain from the previous row. Be sure to insert hook in the center of the "V" (*and back bar*) of the top chain of the turning chain (*see Illustration 37*). Stop and count your double crochet stitches; there should be 12 stitches. Now, turn.

Illustration 37

Here is the way the instructions might be written in a pattern:

Row 2: Ch 3, dc in each dc across, turn. *(12 dc)*

WORKING ROW 3

Row 3 is worked exactly as you worked row 2.

In a pattern, instructions would read:

Row 3: Rep row 2.

For practice, work 3 more rows, repeating row 2. At the end of the last row, fasten off the yarn as you did for the single crochet practice piece. Photo B shows a sample of 6 rows of double crochet and how to count the stitches and rows.

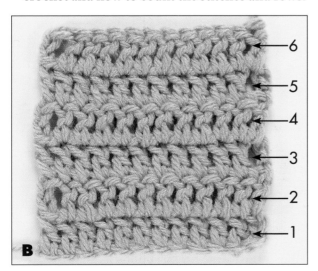

BREAK TIME!

Now you have learned the 2 most often used stitches in crochet. Since you've worked so hard, it's time to take a break. Walk around, relax your hands, have a snack or just take a few minutes to release the stress that sometimes develops when learning something new.

LESSON 6: HALF DOUBLE CROCHET (ABBREVIATED HDC)

Just as its name implies, this stitch eliminates 1 step of double crochet and works up about half as tall.

To practice, chain 13 stitches loosely.

WORKING ROW 1

Step 1: Bring yarn once over hook from back to front, skip the first 2 chains, then insert hook in the 3rd chain from the hook *(see Illustration 38)*.

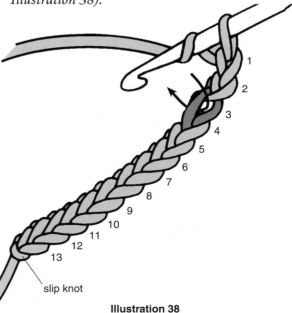

Illustration 38

Remember not to count the loop on the hook as a chain.

Step 2: Hook yarn and pull it through the chain stitch and up onto the working area of the hook. You now have 3 loops on the hook (*see Illustration 39*).

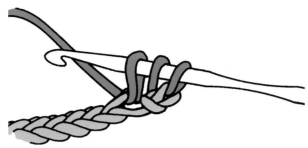

Illustration 39

Step 3: Hook yarn and pull it through all 3 loops on the hook in one motion (*see Illustration 40*).

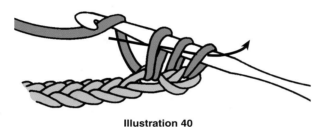

Illustration 40

You have completed 1 half double crochet and 1 loop remains on the hook (*see Illustration 41*).

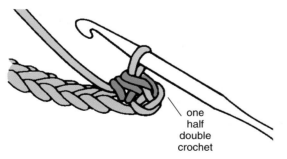

one half double crochet

Illustration 41

In next chain stitch, work a half double crochet as follows:

Step 1: Bring yarn over hook from back to front, insert hook in next chain.

Step 2: Hook yarn and pull it through the chain stitch and up onto the working area of the hook. You now have 3 loops on the hook.

Step 3: Hook yarn and pull it through all 3 loops on the hook in one motion.

Repeat the previous 3 steps in each remaining chain stitch across.

Stop and count your stitches; you should have 12 half double crochets, counting the first 2 chains you skipped at the beginning of the row as a half double crochet (*see Illustration 42*).

Illustration 42

Turn your work.

WORKING ROW 2

Like double crochet, the turning chain counts as a stitch in half double crochet (*unless your pattern specifies otherwise*). Chain 2, skip the first half double crochet of the previous row and work a half double in the 2nd stitch (*see Illustration 43*) and in each remaining stitch across the previous row and turn. At the beg of the row, chain 2.

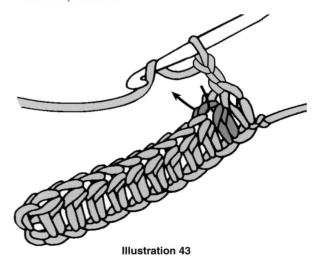

Illustration 43

Here is the way the instructions might be written in a pattern:

Row 2: Ch 2, hdc in each hdc across, turn. (*12 hdc*)

WORKING ROW 3

Row 3 is worked exactly as you worked row 2.

For practice, work 3 more rows, repeating row 2. Be sure to count your stitches carefully at the end of each row. When the practice rows are completed, fasten off. Photo C shows a sample of 6 rows of half double crochet and how to count the stitches and the rows.

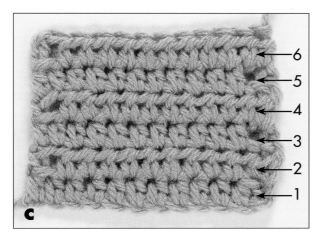

LESSON 7: TREBLE CROCHET (ABBREVIATED TR)

Treble crochet is a tall stitch that works up quickly and is fun to do. To practice, first chain 15 stitches loosely. Then work the first row as follows:

WORKING ROW 1

Step 1: Bring yarn twice over the hook (*from back to front*), skip the first 4 chains, then insert hook into the 5th chain from the hook (*see Illustration 44*).

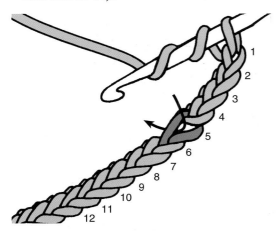

Illustration 44

Step 2: Hook yarn and pull it through the chain stitch and up into the working area of the hook; you now have 4 loops on the hook (*see Illustration 45*).

Illustration 45

Step 3: Hook yarn and pull it through the first 2 loops on the hook (*see Illustration 46*).

Illustration 46

You now have 3 loops on the hook (*see Illustration 46a*).

Illustration 46a

Step 4: Hook yarn again and pull it through the next 2 loops on the hook (*see Illustration 47*).

Illustration 47

2 loops remain on the hook (*see Illustration 47a*).

Illustration 47a

Step 5: Hook yarn and pull it through both remaining loops on the hook (*see Illustration 48*).

Illustration 48

You have now completed 1 treble crochet and 1 loop remains on the hook (*see Illustration 49*).

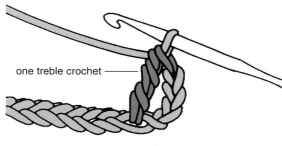

one treble crochet

Illustration 49

In next chain stitch, work a treble crochet as follows:

Step 1: Bring yarn twice over the hook (*from back to front*); insert hook in the next chain (*see Illustration 50*).

Illustration 50

Step 2: Hook yarn and pull it through the chain stitch and up onto the working area of the hook; you now have 4 loops on the hook.

Step 3: Hook yarn and pull it through the first 2 loops on the hook.

You now have 3 loops on the hook.

Step 4: Hook yarn again and pull it through the next 2 loops on the hook.

2 loops remain on the hook.

Step 5: Hook yarn and pull it through both remaining loops on the hook.

Repeat the previous 5 steps in each remaining chain stitch across. When you've worked a treble crochet in the last chain, count your stitches. There should be 12 of them, counting the first 4 chains you skipped at the beginning of the row as a treble crochet (*see Illustration 51*); turn work.

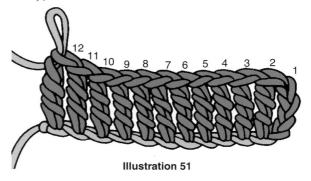

Illustration 51

Hint: In working the first row of treble crochet, the 4 chains skipped before making the first treble crochet are always counted as a treble crochet stitch.

WORKING ROW 2

Chain 4 to bring your yarn up to the correct height, and to count as the first stitch of the row. Skip the first stitch and work a treble crochet in the 2nd stitch *(see Illustration 52).*

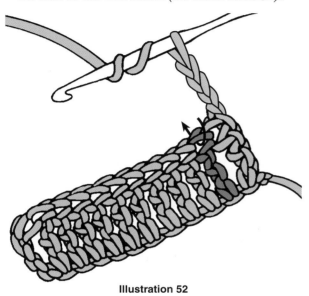

Illustration 52

Work a treble crochet in each remaining stitch across previous row; be sure to work last treble crochet in the top of the turning chain from the previous row. Count stitches: Be sure you still have 12 stitches; turn work.

Hint: Remember to work last treble crochet of each row in turning chain of previous row. Missing this stitch in the turning chain is a common error.

Here is the way the instructions might be written in a pattern:

Row 2: Ch 4, tr in each tr across, turn. *(12 tr)*

WORKING ROW 3

Work row 3 exactly as you worked row 2.

For practice, work 3 more rows, repeating row 2. At the end of the last row, fasten off the yarn. Photo D shows a sample of 6 rows of treble crochet and how to count the stitches and rows.

LESSON 8: DOUBLE TRIPLE (ABBREVIATED DTR)

Double triple is the tallest of the stitches and is also used for increasing. To practice, first chain 16 stitches loosely. Then work the first row as follows:

WORKING ROW 1

Step 1: Bring thread 3 times over the hook (*from back to front*), skip the first 5 chains, then insert hook into the 6th chain from the hook (*see Illustration 53*).

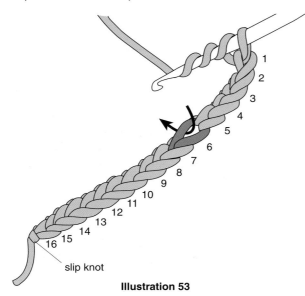

Illustration 53

Step 2: Hook thread and pull it through the chain stitch and up onto the working area of the hook, you now have 5 loops on hook (*see Illustration 54*).

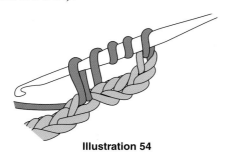

Illustration 54

Step 3: Hook thread and pull it through the first 2 loops on hook (*see Illustration 55*).

Illustration 55

You now have 4 loops on hook (*see Illustration 55a*).

Illustration 55a

Step 4: Hook thread again and pull it through the next 2 loops on the hook (*see Illustration 56*).

Illustration 56

3 loops remain on the hook (*see Illustration 56a*).

Illustration 56a

Step 5: Hook thread again and pull it through the next 2 loops on the hook (*see Illustration 57*).

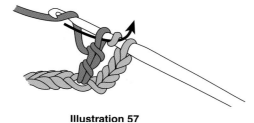

Illustration 57

2 loops remain on the hook (*see Illustration 57a*).

Illustration 57a

Step 6: Hook thread and pull it through both remaining loops on the hook (*see Illustration 58*).

Illustration 58

You have now completed 1 double triple and 1 loop remains on the hook (*see Illustration 59*).

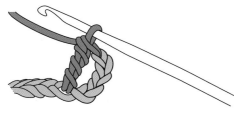

Illustration 59

In next chain stitch work a double triple as follows:

Step 1: Bring thread 3 times over the hook (*from back to front*), insert hook in the next chain (*see Illustration 60*).

Illustration 60

Steps 2–6: Rep the preceding steps 2–6.

Repeat the previous 5 steps in each remaining chain stitch across.

When you've worked a double triple in the last chain, count your stitches; there should be 12, counting the first 5 chains you skipped dc at the beginning of the row as a double triple (*see Illustration 61*).

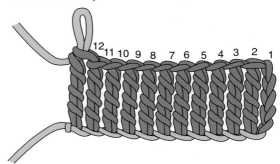

Illustration 61

Now, chain 5 and turn.

For practice, work 3 more rows.

At end of last row, fasten off.

LESSON 9: SLIP STITCH (ABBREVIATED SL ST)

This is the shortest of all crochet stitches and is really more a technique than a stitch. Slip stitches are usually used to move yarn across a group of stitches without adding height, or they may be used to join work.

MOVING YARN ACROSS STITCHES

Chain 10.

WORKING ROW 1

Double crochet in the 4th chain from hook (see Lesson 3 on page 107) and in each chain across. Turn work. On the next row, you are going to slip stitch across the first 4 stitches before beginning to work double crochet again.

WORKING ROW 2

Instead of making 3 chains for the turning chain as you would usually do for a 2nd row of double crochet, this time just chain 1. The turning chain-1 does not count as a stitch; therefore, insert hook under both loops of first stitch, hook yarn and pull it through both loops of stitch and loop on the hook (see Illustration 62); 1 slip stitch made.

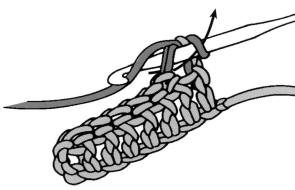

Illustration 62

Work a slip stitch in the same manner in each of the next 3 stitches. Now we're going to finish the row in double crochet; chain 3 to get yarn at the right height (the chain-3 counts as a double crochet), then work a double crochet in each of the remaining stitches. Look at your work and see how we moved the yarn across with slip stitches, adding very little height (see Illustration 63).

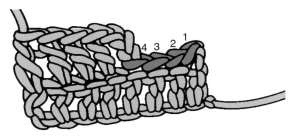

Illustration 63

Fasten off and save the sample.

Here is the way the instructions might be written in a pattern.

Row 2: Sl st in each of first 4 dc, ch 3, dc in each rem dc across. Fasten off. (5 dc)

Hint: When slip stitching across stitches, always work very loosely.

JOINING STITCHES
JOINING A CHAIN INTO A CIRCLE

Chain 6, then insert hook through the first chain you made (next to the slip knot—Illustration 64).

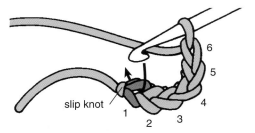

Illustration 64

Hook yarn and pull it through the chain and through the loop on hook; you have now joined the 6 chains into a circle or a ring. This is the way many motifs, such as granny squares, are started. Cut yarn and keep this practice piece as a sample.

JOINING THE END OF A ROUND TO THE BEGINNING OF THE SAME ROUND

Chain 6, join with a slip stitch in first chain you made to form a ring. Chain 3, work 11 double crochet in the ring, insert hook in 3rd chain of beginning chain 3 (see Illustration 65); hook yarn and pull it through the chain and through the loop on the hook; you have now joined the round. Cut yarn and keep this piece as a sample.

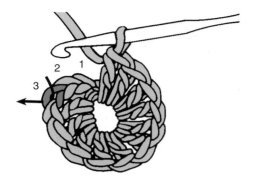

Illustration 65

Here is the way the instructions might be written in a pattern:

Rnd 1: Ch 3, 11 dc in ring, join with sl st in 3rd ch of beg ch-3.

LESSON 10: STITCH SAMPLER

Now you've learned the basic stitches of crochet! Wasn't it fun? The hard part is over!

To help you understand the difference in the way single crochet, half double crochet, double crochet, treble crochet and double triple stitches are worked, and the difference in their heights, let's make 1 more sample.

Chain 17 loosely. Taking care not to work too tightly, single crochet in the 2nd chain from hook and in each of the next 3 chains, work a half double crochet in each of the next 4 chains, work a double crochet in each of the next 4 chains, work a treble crochet in each of the next 4 chains. Fasten off. Your work should look like Photo E.

E

LESSON 11: WORKING WITH COLORS

Working with colors often involves reading charts, changing colors and learning how to carry or pick up colors.

WORKING FROM CHARTS

Charts are easy to work from once you understand how to follow them. When working from a chart, remember that for each odd-numbered row, you will work the chart from right to left and for each even-numbered row, you will work the chart from left to right.

Odd-numbered rows are worked on the right side of the piece and even-numbered rows are worked on the wrong side. To help follow across the row, you will find it helpful to place a ruler or sheet of paper directly below the row being worked.

CHANGING COLORS

To change from working color to a new color, work the last stitch to be done in the working color until two loops remain on the hook (*Photo A*). Pull new color through the 2 loops on hook. Drop working color (*Photo B*) and continue to work in the new color. This method can be used when change of color is at the end of a row or within the row.

A

B

CARRYING OR PICKING UP COLORS

In some patterns, you may need to carry a color on the wrong side of the work for several stitches or pick up a color used on the previous row. To carry a color means to carry the strand on the wrong side of the work. To prevent having loops of unworked yarn, it is helpful to work over the strand of the carried color. To do this, consider the strand a part of the stitch being worked into and simply insert the hook in the stitch and pull the new color through (*Photo C*). When changing from working color to a color that has been carried or used on the previous row, always bring this color under the working color. This is very important, as it prevents holes in your work.

LESSON 12: WORKING WITH CROCHET COTTON

To work with crochet cotton, you will need a steel hook and some crochet cotton.

THREAD

Crochet thread comes in many sizes, ranging from very fine crochet cotton (sizes 80 and 100), used for lace-making and tatting, to sizes 30, 20 and 10, used for doilies and bedspreads. The larger the number, the thinner the thread. The most commonly used thread is size 10, and it is often called bedspread weight. It is readily available in white, ecru and cream, as well as a wide variety of colors. As with yarn labels, always read thread labels carefully. The label will tell you how much thread is in the skein or ball in ounces, grams, meters or yards; the type of thread, usually cotton; and washability. Also, there is usually a dye-lot number. This number assures you that the color of each ball with this number is the same. Thread with the same color name may vary from dye lot to dye lot, creating variations in color when a project is completed. Therefore, when purchasing thread for a project, it is important to match the dye-lot number on the balls.

To weave in thread ends, a size 18 steel tapestry needle works well.

HOOKS

Steel hooks are sized numerically from 16 (*smallest*) to 0, and are about 5 inches long, which is shorter than aluminum or plastic hooks. Their shape is different from other crochet hooks. There is the throat, then the shank, and after the shank, the steel begins to widen again before it reaches the fingerhold (*see Illustration 66*).

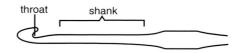

Illustration 66

When crocheting, it is important that the stitches do not slide beyond the shank as this will cause a loose tension and alter the gauge. If you find you are having difficulty at first, place a piece of tape around the hook to keep the stitches from sliding past the correct area. With practice, you will work in the right place automatically.

special helps

INCREASING & DECREASING

Shaping is done by increasing, that is, adding stitches to make the crocheted piece wider, or decreasing, subtracting stitches to make the piece narrower.

Note: *Make a practice sample by chaining 15 stitches loosely and working 4 rows of single crochet with 14 stitches in each row. Do not fasten off at end of last row. Use this sample swatch to practice the following method of increasing stitches.*

INCREASING

To increase 1 stitch in single, half double, double or treble crochet, simply work 2 stitches in 1 stitch. For example, if you are working in single crochet and you need to increase 1 stitch, you would work 1 single crochet in the next stitch, then you would work another single crochet in the same stitch.

For practice: On sample swatch, turn work and chain 1. Single crochet in each of first 2 stitches, increase in next stitch by working 2 single crochets in stitch *(see Illustration 67)*.

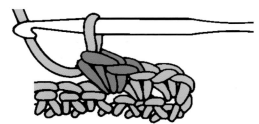

single crochet increase

Illustration 67

Repeat increase in each stitch across row to last 2 stitches, single crochet in each of next 2 stitches. Count your stitches—you should have 24 stitches. If you don't have 24

stitches, examine your swatch to see if you have increased in each specified stitch. Rework the row if necessary.

Increases in half double, double and treble crochet are shown in Illustrations 67a, 67b and 67c.

half double crochet increase

Illustration 67a

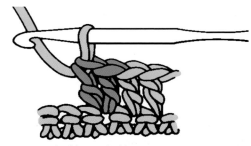

double crochet increase

Illustration 67b

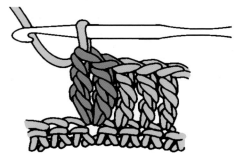

treble crochet increase

Illustration 67c

Note: Make another practice sample by chaining 15 loosely and working 4 rows of single crochet. Do not fasten off at end of last row. Use this sample swatch to practice the following methods of decreasing stitches.

DECREASING

This is how to work a decrease in the 4 main stitches. Each decrease gives 1 fewer stitch than you had before.

Single crochet decrease (sc dec): Insert hook and pull up a loop in each of the next 2 stitches *(3 loops now on hook)*, hook yarn and pull through all 3 loops on the hook *(see Illustration 68)*.

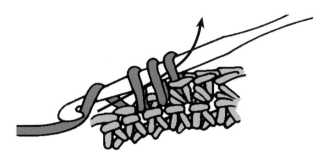

Illustration 68

Single crochet decrease made *(see Illustration 69)*.

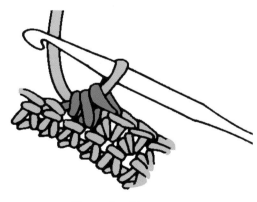

Illustration 69

Double crochet decrease (dc dec): Work a double crochet in the specified stitch until 2 loops remain on the hook *(see Illustration 70)*.

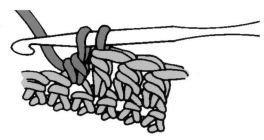

Illustration 70

Keeping these 2 loops on hook, work another double crochet in the next stitch until 3 loops remain on hook, hook yarn and pull through all 3 loops on the hook *(see Illustration 71)*.

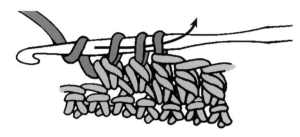

Illustration 71

Double crochet decrease made *(see Illustration 72)*.

Illustration 72

Half double crochet decrease (hdc dec): Yarn over, insert hook in specified stitch and pull up a loop—3 loops on the hook *(see Illustration 73)*.

Illustration 73

Keeping these 3 loops on hook, yarn over and pull up a loop in the next stitch *(5 loops now on hook)*, hook yarn and pull through all 5 loops on the hook *(see Illustration 74)*.

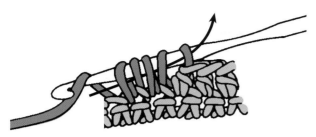

Illustration 74

Half double crochet decrease made *(see Illustration 75)*.

Illustration 75

Treble crochet decrease (tr dec): Work a treble crochet in the specified stitch until 2 loops remain on the hook *(see Illustration 76)*.

Illustration 76

Keeping these 2 loops on hook, work another triple crochet in the next stitch until 3 loops remain on the hook, hook yarn and pull through all loops on the hook *(see Illustration 77)*.

Illustration 77

Treble crochet decrease made *(see Illustration 78)*.

Illustration 78

JOINING NEW THREAD

Never tie or leave knots! In crochet, yarn ends can be easily worked in and hidden because of the density of the stitches. Always leave at least 6-inch ends when fastening off yarn just used and when joining new yarn. If a flaw or a knot appears in the yarn while you are working from a skein, cut out the imperfection and rejoin the yarn.

Whenever possible, join new yarn at the end of a row. To do this, work the last stitch with the old yarn until 2 loops remain on the hook, then with the new yarn complete the stitch *(see Illustration 79)*.

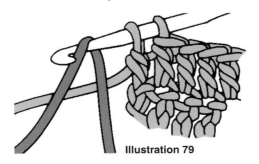

Illustration 79

To join new yarn in the middle of a row, when about 12 inches of the old yarn remains, work several more stitches with the old yarn, working the stitches over the end of new yarn (*Illustration 80 is shown in double crochet*). Then change yarns in stitch as previously explained.

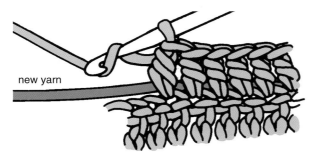

Illustration 80

Continuing with the new yarn, work the following stitches over the old yarn end.

FINISHING

A carefully crocheted project can be disappointing if the finishing has been done incorrectly. Correct finishing techniques are not difficult, but do require time, attention and knowledge of basic techniques.

WEAVING IN ENDS

The first procedure of finishing is to securely weave in all yarn ends. Thread a size 16 steel tapestry needle with yarn, then weave running stitches either horizontally or vertically on the wrong side of work. First weave about 1 inch in one direction and then ½ inch in the reverse direction. Be sure yarn doesn't show on right side of work. Cut off excess yarn. Never weave in more than 1 yarn end at a time.

SEWING SEAMS

Edges in crochet are usually butted together f or seaming instead of layered, to avoid bulk. Do not sew too tightly—seams should be elastic and have the same stretch as the crocheted pieces.

Carefully matching stitches and rows as much as possible, sew the seams with the same yarn you used when crocheting.

Invisible seam: This seam provides a smooth, neat appearance because the edges are woven together invisibly from the right side. Join vertical edges, such as side or sleeve seams, through the matching edge stitches, bringing the yarn up through the posts of the stitches (*see Illustration 81*).

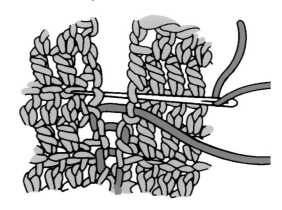

Illustration 81

If a firmer seam is desired, weave the edges together through both the tops and the posts of the matching edge stitches.

Backstitch seam: This method gives a strong, firm edge and is used when the seam will have a lot of stress or pull on it. Hold the pieces with right sides together and then sew through both thicknesses as shown (*see Illustration 82*).

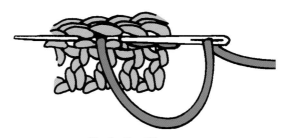

Illustration 82

Overcast seam: Strips and pieces of afghans are frequently joined in this manner. Hold the pieces with right sides together and overcast edges, carefully matching stitches on the two pieces (*see Illustration 83*).

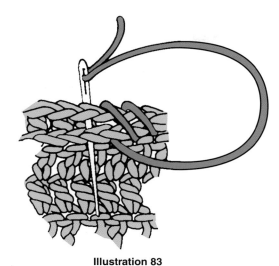

Illustration 83

Edges can also be joined in this manner, using only the back loops or the front loops of each stitch (*see illustration 88 on page 129*).

Crocheted seam: Holding pieces with right sides together, join yarn with a slip stitch at right-side edge. Loosely slip stitch pieces together, being sure not to pull stitches too tightly (*see Illustration 84*). You may wish to use a hook one size larger than the one used in the project.

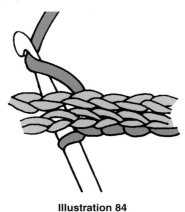

Illustration 84

EDGING

SINGLE CROCHET EDGING:

A row of single crochet worked around a completed project gives a finished look. The instructions will say to "work a row of single crochet, taking care to keep work flat." This means you need to adjust your stitches as you work. To work the edging, insert hook from front to back through the edge stitch and work a single crochet. Continue evenly along the

edge. You may need to skip a row or a stitch here or there to keep the edging from rippling or add a stitch to keep the work from pulling.

When working around a corner, it is usually necessary to work at least three stitches in the corner center stitch to keep the corner flat and square (*see Illustration 85*).

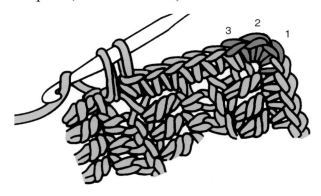

Illustration 85

REVERSE SINGLE CROCHET EDGING

A single crochet edging is sometimes worked from left to right for a more dominant edge. To work reverse single crochet, insert hook in stitch to the right (*see Illustration 86*), hook yarn and draw through stitch, hook yarn and draw through both loops on the hook (*see Illustration 87*).

Illustration 86

Illustration 87

crochet basics
reading patterns

ABBREVIATIONS

Crochet patterns are written in a special language full of abbreviations, asterisks, parentheses, brackets and other symbols and terms. These short forms are used so instructions will not take up too much space. They may seem confusing at first, but once understood, they are really easy to follow.

ABBREVIATIONS

beg . . . . . begin/begins/beginning	**inc** . . .increase/increases/increasing
bpdc . . . .back post double crochet	**lp(s)** . . . . loop(s)
bpsc . . . . . back post single crochet	**MC** . . . . .main color
bptr . . . . . .back post treble crochet	**mm** . . . . millimeter(s)
CC . . . . .contrasting color	**oz** . . . . ounce(s)
ch(s) . . . . .chain(s)	**pc** . . . . .popcorn(s)
ch- . . . . refers to chain or space	**rem** . . . . . remain/remains/remaining
previously made (i.e., ch-1 space)	**rep(s)** . . . . repeat(s)
ch sp(s) . . . . chain space(s)	**rnd(s)** . . . . .round(s)
cl(s) . . . . cluster(s)	**RS** . . . . .right side
cm . . . . .centimeter(s)	**sc** . . . . .single crochet
dc . . double crochet (singular/plural)	(singular/plural)
dc dec . . . . .double crochet	**sc dec** . . . . .single crochet
2 or more stitches together,	2 or more stitches together,
as indicated	as indicated
dec . . . . decrease/decreases/	**sk** . . . . skip/skipped/skipping
decreasing	**sl st(s)** . . . . .slip stitch(es)
dtr. . . . . .double treble crochet	**sp(s)** . . . . space(s)/spaced
ext . . . . extended	**st(s)** . . . . stitch(es)
fpdc . . . . front post double crochet	**tog** . . . . together
fpsc . . . . . . front post single crochet	**tr** . . . . .treble crochet
fptr . . . . . front post treble crochet	**trtr** . . . . triple treble
g . . . . gram(s)	**WS** . . . . wrong side
hdc . . . . half double crochet	**yd(s)** . . . . yard(s)
hdc dec . . . . . . half double crochet	**yo** . . . . yarn over
2 or more stitches together,	
as indicated	

SYMBOLS

An asterisk is used to mark the beginning of a portion of instructions which will be worked more than once; thus, "rep from * twice" means after working the instructions once, repeat the instructions following the asterisk twice more (*3 times in all*).

[ ] Brackets are used to enclose instructions which should be repeated the number of times specified immediately following the brackets: "[2 sc in next dc, sc in next dc] twice." Brackets are also used to indicate additional or clarifying information for multiple sizes: "Child's size 2 [4, 6]"; "Row 29 [31, 33]."

( ) Parentheses are used to set off and clarify a group of stitches that are to be worked all into the same space or stitch, such as: "(2 dc, ch 1, 2 dc) in corner sp."

{ } Braces are used to indicate a set of repeat instructions within a bracketed or parenthetical set of repeat instructions: "[{Ch 5, sc in next shell sp} twice, ch 5, sk next dc]"; "({dc, ch 1} 5 times, dc) in next ch sp."

TERMS

Front loop (front lp) is the loop toward you at the top of the stitch (*see Illustration 88*).

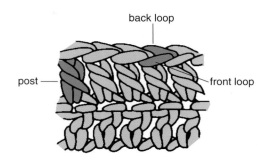

back loop

post — front loop

Illustration 88

Back loop (back lp) is the loop away from you at the top of the stitch (*see Illustration 88*).

Post is the vertical part of the stitch (*see Illustration 88*).

Work even means to continue to work in the pattern as established, without increasing or decreasing.

Wrong side (WS): The side of the work that will not show when project is in use.

Right side (RS): The side that will show when project is in use.

Right-hand side: The side nearest your right hand as you are working.

Left-hand side: The side nearest your left hand as you are working.

Right front: The piece of a garment that will be worn on the right-hand side of the body.

Left front: The piece of a garment that will be worn on the left-hand side of the body.

crochet basics

gauge

We've left this until last, but it really is the single most important thing in crochet.

If you don't work to gauge, your crocheted projects may not be the correct size, and you may not have enough yarn to finish out project.

Gauge means the number of stitches per inch and rows per inch that result from a specified yarn worked with a specific-size hook. Since everyone crochets differently—some loosely, some tightly, some in-between—the measurements of individual work can vary greatly when using the same-size hook and yarn. It is your responsibility to make sure you achieve the gauge specified in the pattern.

Hook sizes given in instructions are merely guides and should never be used without making a 4-inch-square sample swatch to check gauge. Make the sample gauge swatch using the size hook, yarn and stitch specified in the pattern. If you have more stitches per inch than specified, try again using a smaller-size hook. If you have fewer stitches per inch than specified, try again using a larger-size hook. Do not hesitate to change to a larger- or smaller-size

hook, if necessary, to achieve gauge. If you have the correct number of stitches per inch, but cannot achieve the row gauge, adjust the height of your stitches. This means that after inserting the hook to begin a new stitch, draw up a little more yarn if your stitches are not tall enough—this makes the first loop slightly higher; or draw up less yarn if your stitches are too tall. Practice will help you achieve the correct height.

This photo shows how to measure your gauge.

metric conversion charts

INCHES INTO MILLIMETRES & CENTIMETRES (Rounded off slightly)

inches	mm	cm	inches	cm	inches	cm	inches	cm
1/8	3	0.3	5	12.5	21	53.5	38	96.5
1/4	6	0.6	5 1/2	14	22	56	39	99
3/8	10	1	6	15	23	58.5	40	101.5
1/2	13	1.3	7	18	24	61	41	104
5/8	15	1.5	8	20.5	25	63.5	42	106.5
3/4	20	2	9	23	26	66	43	109
7/8	22	2.2	10	25.5	27	68.5	44	112
1	25	2.5	11	28	28	71	45	114.5
1 1/4	32	3.2	12	30.5	29	73.5	46	117
1 1/2	38	3.8	13	33	30	76	47	119.5
1 3/4	45	4.5	14	35.5	31	79	48	122
2	50	5	15	38	32	81.5	49	124.5
2 1/2	65	6.5	16	40.5	33	84	50	127
3	75	7.5	17	43	34	86.5		
3 1/2	90	9	18	46	35	89		
4	100	10	19	48.5	36	91.5		
4 1/2	115	11.5	20	51	37	94		

KNITTING NEEDLES CONVERSION CHART

Canada/U.S.	0	1	2	3	4	5	6	7	8	9	10	10½	11	13	15
Metric (mm)	2	2¼	2¾	3¼	3½	3¾	4	4½	5	5½	6	6½	8	9	10

CROCHET HOOKS CONVERSION CHART

Canada/U.S.	1/B	2/C	3/D	4/E	5/F	6/G	8/H	9/I	10/J	10½/K	N
Metric (mm)	2.25	2.75	3.25	3.5	3.75	4.25	5	5.5	6	6.5	9.0

METRIC CONVERSIONS

yards	x	.9144	=	metres (m)
yards	x	91.44	=	centimetres (cm)
inches	x	2.54	=	centimetres (cm)
inches	x	25.40	=	millimetres (mm)
inches	x	.0254	=	metres (m)

centimetres	x	.3937	=	inches
metres	x	1.0936	=	yards

crochet basics
skill levels

■□□□ BEGINNER

Beginner projects for first-time crocheters using basic stitches. Minimal shaping.

■■□□ EASY

Easy projects using basic stitches, repetitive stitch patterns, simple color changes and simple shaping and finishing.

■■■□ INTERMEDIATE

Intermediate projects with a variety of stitches, mid-level shaping and finishing.

■■■■ EXPERIENCED

Experienced projects using advanced techniques and stitches, detailed shaping and refined finishing.

standard yarn weights

Categories of yarn, gauge ranges, and recommended needle and hook sizes

Yarn Weight Symbol & Category Names	1 SUPER FINE	2 FINE	3 LIGHT	4 MEDIUM	5 BULKY	6 SUPER BULKY
Type of Yarns in Category	Sock, Fingering, Baby	Sport, Baby	DK, Light Worsted	Worsted, Afghan, Aran	Chunky, Craft, Rug	Super Chunky, Roving
Crochet Gauge* Ranges in Single Crochet to 4 inch	21–32 sts	16–20 sts	12–17 sts	11–14 sts	8–11 sts	5–9 sts
Recommended Hook in Metric Size Range	2.25–3.5 mm	3.5–4.5 mm	4.5–5.5 mm	5.5–6.5 mm	6.5–9 mm	9 mm and larger
Recommended Hook U.S. Size Range	B-1–E-4	E-4–7	7–I-9	I-9–K-10½	K-10½–M-13	M-13 and larger

* GUIDELINES ONLY: The above reflect the most commonly used gauges and hook sizes for specific yarn categories.

STITCH GUIDE

FOR MORE COMPLETE INFORMATION, VISIT FREEPATTERNS.COM

STITCH ABBREVIATIONS

beg .... begin/begins/beginning
bpdc .... back post double crochet
bpsc .... back post single crochet
bptr .... back post treble crochet
CC .... contrasting color
ch(s) .... chain(s)
ch- ...,........... refers to chain or space
previously made (i.e., ch-1 space)
ch sp(s) .... chain space(s)
cl(s) .... cluster(s)
cm .... centimeter(s)
dc .... double crochet (singular/plural)
dc dec .... double crochet 2 or more
stitches together, as indicated
dec............... decrease/decreases/decreasing
dtr .... double treble crochet
ext ....extended
fpdc.......................... front post double crochet
fpsc .... front post single crochet
fptr .... front post treble crochet
g .... gram(s)
hdc .... half double crochet
hdc dec .... half double crochet 2 or more
stitches together, as indicated
inc .... increase/increases/increasing
lp(s)..loop(s)
MC ....main color
mm .... millimeter(s)
oz.. ounce(s)
pc ....popcorn(s)
rem .... remain/remains/remaining
rep(s) ....repeat(s)
rnd(s) ....round(s)
RS .... right side
sc .... single crochet (singular/plural)
sc dec .... single crochet 2 or more
stitches together, as indicated
sk ....skip/skipped/skipping
sl st(s) .... slip stitch(es)
sp(s) .... space(s)/spaced
st(s) .... stitch(es)
tog ....together
tr .... treble crochet
trtr...triple treble
WS .... wrong side
yd(s) ....yard(s)
yo .... yarn over

YARN CONVERSION

OUNCES TO GRAMS		GRAMS TO OUNCES	
1	28.4	25	⅞
2	56.7	40	1⅔
3	85.0	50	1¾
4	113.4	100	3½

UNITED STATES — UNITED KINGDOM

UNITED STATES		UNITED KINGDOM
sl st (slip stitch)	=	sc (single crochet)
sc (single crochet)	=	dc (double crochet)
hdc (half double crochet)	=	htr (half treble crochet)
dc (double crochet)	=	tr (treble crochet)
tr (treble crochet)	=	dtr (double treble crochet)
dtr (double treble crochet)	=	ttr (triple treble crochet)
skip	=	miss

Reverse Single Crochet (reverse sc): Ch 1. Skip first st. [Working from left to right, insert hook in next st from front to back, draw up lp on hook, yo, and draw through both lps on hook.]

Chain (ch): Yo, pull through lp on hook.

Single crochet (sc): Insert hook in st, yo, pull through st, yo, pull through both lps on hook.

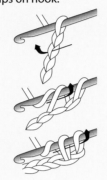

Double crochet (dc): Yo, insert hook in st, yo, pull through st, [yo, pull through 2 lps] twice.

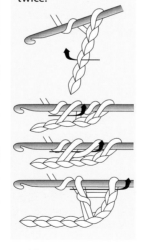

Front loop (front lp) Back loop (back lp)
Front Loop Back Loop

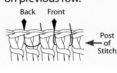

Front post stitch (fp): Back post stitch (bp): When working post st, insert hook from right to left around post st on previous row.

Back   Front

Post of Stitch

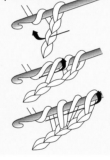

Half double crochet (hdc): Yo, insert hook in st, yo, pull through st, yo, pull through all 3 lps on hook.

Double treble crochet (dtr): Yo 3 times, insert hook in st, yo, pull through st, [yo, pull through 2 lps] 4 times.

Slip stitch (sl st): Insert hook in st, pull through both lps on hook.

Chain Color Change (ch color change) Yo with new color, draw through last lp on hook.

Double Crochet Color Change (dc color change) Drop first color, yo with new color, draw through last 2 lps of st.

Treble crochet (tr): Yo twice, insert hook in st, yo, pull through st, [yo, pull through 2 lps] 3 times.

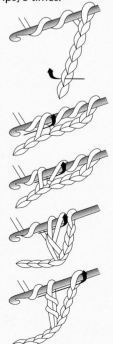

Single crochet decrease (sc dec): (Insert hook, yo, draw lp through) in each of the sts indicated, yo, draw through all lps on hook.

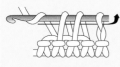

Example of 2-sc dec

Half double crochet decrease (hdc dec): (Yo, insert hook in st, yo, draw lp through) in each of the sts indicated, yo, draw through all lps on hook.

Example of 2-hdc dec

Double crochet decrease (dc dec): (Yo, insert hook, yo, draw loop through, yo, draw through 2 lps on hook) in each of the sts indicated, yo, draw through all lps on hook.

Example of 2-dc dec

Treble crochet decrease (tr dec): Holding back last lp of each st, tr in each of the sts indicated, yo, pull through all lps on hook.

Example of 2-tr dec

HOUSE of
WHITE
BIRCHES

PUBLISHERS
SINCE 1947

Crochet Compendium is published by DRG, 306 East Parr Road, Berne, IN 46711.
Printed in USA. Copyright © 2011 DRG. All rights reserved. This publication may not be
reproduced in part or in whole without written permission from the publisher.

RETAIL STORES: If you would like to carry this pattern book or any other
DRG publications, visit DRGwholesale.com

Every effort has been made to ensure that the instructions in this publication are complete and accurate.
We cannot, however, take responsibility for human error, typographical mistakes or variations
in individual work. Please visit AnniesCustomerCare.com to check for pattern updates..

ISBN: 978-1-59217-341-9

1 2 3 4 5 6 7 8 9